NEW JERSEY TEST PREP

Reading Comprehension

Common Core Workbook

Grade 7

ISBN 978-1500854324

CONTENTS

INTRODUCTION
For Parents, Teachers, and Tutors

About the Book

This workbook will develop the reading comprehension skills that students are expected to have, while preparing students for the state tests. This workbook covers the skills listed in the Common Core State Standards. The focus of the book is on developing reading comprehension skills, but the complementary writing and language skills are also covered.

Ongoing Reading Comprehension Practice

The aim of this book is to give students ongoing reading comprehension practice without the stress of long passages and question sets. Each set contains four short texts with questions, or two texts in paired sets. By completing each set, students will gain experience with a range of passage types, become familiar with common question types, practice understanding and responding to texts, develop confidence, and master Common Core reading skills.

Developing Common Core Reading Skills

The state of New Jersey has adopted the Common Core State Standards. These standards describe what students are expected to know. The reading standards are divided into two areas: Reading Standards for Literature and Reading Standards for Informational Text. This workbook includes sets that focus only on literature, only on informational texts, and mixed sets that cover both. The workbook also includes sets with paired passages, where students synthesize and integrate information from two texts.

Introducing Core Skills

Each passage in this workbook includes a Core Skills Practice exercise that focuses on one key reading, writing, or language skill. These exercises will introduce students to the key skills and help students transition to the more challenging Common Core standards.

Preparing for the PARCC English Language Arts Assessment

Students will be assessed each year by taking a set of tests known as the PARCC assessments. This workbook will help prepare students for these assessments. The reading comprehension skills developed are those that will be assessed, so the strong skill development gained will help students perform well on the assessments. The workbook also provides experience understanding, analyzing, and responding to passages, as well as practice answering selected-response and constructed-response questions.

Reading Comprehension

Set 1

Literary Texts

Instructions

Read each passage. Complete the exercise under each passage.

Then complete the questions following each passage. For each multiple-choice question, fill in the circle for the correct answer. For other types of questions, follow the instructions given. Some of the questions require a written answer. Write your answer on the lines provided.

Not a Farmer's Day

It was a sunny afternoon in outback Springwater. Noah, a run-down farmer, was slumped over on a bale of hay in his barn having a nap. Suddenly, a loud crash woke him from his slumber. "What is it now?" Noah grumbled.

He let out a huff and started storming toward the barn door. Stepping outside, he furrowed his brow as the sun struck his weathered face. Slowly his sleepy eyes began to focus and Noah let out a gasp as he saw what all the fuss was about. Noah must have been so tired he forgot to put the brakes on his tractor properly. It had rolled right over the top of his brand new chicken coop. He sighed as he realized that he was only tired because he had spent the whole weekend working tirelessly on the chicken coop.

CORE SKILLS PRACTICE

Many stories involve cause and effect. The cause is the reason for something. The effect is what happens. Answer the questions about cause and effect.

Why does Noah forget to set the brakes on his tractor?

_____

_____

_____

What effect does forgetting to put the brakes on have?

_____

_____

_____

---

1   The word <u>slumped</u> mainly suggests that the farmer was —

   Ⓐ   bored

   Ⓑ   exhausted

   Ⓒ   cranky

   Ⓓ   lazy

2   Why does Noah most likely gasp?

   Ⓐ   He did not realize it was so late.

   Ⓑ   His chicken coop has been destroyed.

   Ⓒ   He thinks his tractor has been stolen.

   Ⓓ   He knows he shouldn't have been sleeping.

3   Which detail about Noah best shows that he is an old farmer?

   Ⓐ   He is having a nap.

   Ⓑ   He has a new chicken coop.

   Ⓒ   He has a weathered face.

   Ⓓ   He is woken by a loud crash.

4   Which statement best explains the irony in the passage?

   Ⓐ   An old tractor destroys a new chicken coop.

   Ⓑ   A chicken coop is destroyed while a farmer naps.

   Ⓒ   The farmer's tiredness from building the chicken coop is the reason it is destroyed.

   Ⓓ   A farmer is unable to get some sleep because of the sound of the tractor knocking down his chicken coop.

The Violet
By Jane Taylor

Down in a green and shady bed
A modest violet grew;
Its stalk was bent, it hung its head,
As if to hide from view.

And yet it was a lovely flower,
No colors bright and fair;
It might have graced a rosy bower,
Instead of hiding there.

Yet there it was content to bloom,
In modest tints arrayed;
And there diffused its sweet perfume,
Within the silent shade.

Then let me to the valley go,
This pretty flower to see;
That I may also learn to grow
In sweet humility.

CORE SKILLS PRACTICE

The author uses many adjectives to describe the violet. List **three** of the adjectives below. Then describe what they all have in common.

1. _____   2. _____   3. _____

_____

_____

_____

1 Which literary device is used to help readers understand the violet?

> **Its stalk was bent, it hung its head,**
> **As if to hide from view.**

Ⓐ Personification, giving an object human emotions

Ⓑ Metaphor, comparing an object with something else

Ⓒ Symbolism, using an object to stand for something else

Ⓓ Hyperbole, using exaggeration to make a point

2 What is the rhyme pattern of each stanza of the poem?

Ⓐ The second and third lines rhyme.

Ⓑ There are two pairs of rhyming lines.

Ⓒ The first and last lines rhyme.

Ⓓ None of the lines rhyme.

3 The main theme of the poem is about being –

Ⓐ hidden

Ⓑ humble

Ⓒ beautiful

Ⓓ natural

4 What feeling is created by the alliteration in the words "silent shade"?

Ⓐ Somberness and concern

Ⓑ Uncertainty and tension

Ⓒ Quietness and calm

Ⓓ Excitement and joy

A Challenge

March 8

Dear Diary,

I've been trying for months now to solve the Rubik's Cube that Dad bought me last year as a birthday present. He knows that collecting odd and zany things is a fun hobby for me. That's one of the reasons I liked it so much.

All you have to do to solve it is get the nine little squares on each side the same color. It sounds simple, but believe me when I tell you that it is not! No matter how many times I turn it here and there, I just can't solve this Rubik's Cube! I've made a pretty pattern out of it, but haven't come close to solving it. I will just have to try again tomorrow.

Bye for now,

Reggie

CORE SKILLS PRACTICE

How do you think Reggie feels about being unable to solve the Rubik's Cube?

_____

_____

_____

_____

_____

---

1   Which two words from the passage have about the same meaning?

Ⓐ   Solve, reasons

Ⓑ   Present, collecting

Ⓒ   Odd, zany

Ⓓ   Pretty, pattern

2   What will Reggie most likely do with the Rubik's Cube?

Ⓐ   Give it to a friend

Ⓑ   Give up and throw it away

Ⓒ   Keep trying until he solves it

Ⓓ   Give it back to his father

3   What does the picture most help the reader understand?

Ⓐ   What a Rubik's Cube is

Ⓑ   Where Reggie got the Rubik's Cube

Ⓒ   How Reggie feels about the Rubik's Cube

Ⓓ   How hard the Rubik's Cube is to solve

4   Which word best describes the tone of the passage?

Ⓐ   Casual

Ⓑ   Questioning

Ⓒ   Frustrated

Ⓓ   Bitter

The New Boy

Lionel sat and stared at his mother in the kitchen. "But why would I want to do that?" he asked with a befuddled look.

His mother chuckled quietly and just smiled. Lionel had just finished telling his mother that a new kid had started at the school that day. He had explained that the boy dressed strangely, had a weird haircut, and didn't seem to fit in with anyone at his school. His mother had suggested that he should make friends with that boy.

"You should make an effort to get to know everybody," his mother said. "You won't know what he's like until you give him a chance. And think about how he must feel. What if that other boy was you?"

Lionel sat and thought about it for a while. He realized that it would mean a lot to him if someone tried to make friends with him, or at least talked to him. He decided that his mother had a good point.

CORE SKILLS PRACTICE

A summary is a description of the events of a story. A summary should include only the main events from the story. Write a summary of "The New Boy."

_____

_____

_____

_____

_____

1   In the first paragraph, what does the word <u>befuddled</u> most likely mean?

    Ⓐ   Patient

    Ⓑ   Embarrassed

    Ⓒ   Puzzled

    Ⓓ   Irritated

2   Which statement describes the main theme of the passage?

    Ⓐ   Starting a new school can be challenging.

    Ⓑ   It is important to have many friends.

    Ⓒ   It is worthwhile to ask others for advice.

    Ⓓ   You should treat others as you wish to be treated.

3   What would Lionel most likely do at school the next day?

    Ⓐ   Ask his friends what they think of the new boy

    Ⓑ   Ignore the new boy

    Ⓒ   Start a conversation with the new boy

    Ⓓ   Observe the new boy more closely

4   Which phrase best describes how Lionel changes in the passage?

    Ⓐ   From cruel to kind

    Ⓑ   From thoughtless to considerate

    Ⓒ   From concerned to relieved

    Ⓓ   From shy to outgoing

5   What message does the passage have about judging people? Use information from the passage to support your answer.

_____

_____

_____

_____

_____

_____

_____

_____

_____

_____

_____

_____

_____

_____

Reading Comprehension

Set 2

Informational Texts

Instructions

Read each passage. Complete the exercise under each passage.

Then complete the questions following each passage. For each multiple-choice question, fill in the circle for the correct answer. For other types of questions, follow the instructions given. Some of the questions require a written answer. Write your answer on the lines provided.

Many Moons

Saturn has many different and diverse moons. They range from moonlets less than a mile across to the enormous moon known as Titan. Titan is actually larger than the planet Mercury, and is even larger than the Earth's moon.

In total, amongst all the debris that makes up Saturn's ring, Saturn has a staggering 62 moons. Of these, 53 have been given names. Most of the major moons are named after mythological figures associated with the Roman god of agriculture and harvest, Saturn.

Saturn's Five Largest Moons

Name	Diameter (kilometers)
Titan	5,150
Rhea	1,527
Lapetus	1,470
Dione	1,123
Enceladus	504

CORE SKILLS PRACTICE

Read this sentence from the passage.

Titan is actually larger than the planet Mercury, and is even larger than the Earth's moon.

Describe a diagram the author could include to make this information clearer.

_____

_____

_____

1   What does the word <u>moonlet</u> most likely mean?

    Ⓐ   A young moon

    Ⓑ   A very small moon

    Ⓒ   A moon that is very far away

    Ⓓ   A moon that is orbiting Saturn

2   How is the first paragraph mainly organized?

    Ⓐ   A problem is described and then a solution is given.

    Ⓑ   Events are described in the order they occur.

    Ⓒ   Facts are given to support an argument.

    Ⓓ   A question is asked and then answered.

3   Which conclusion can be drawn from the information in the table?

    Ⓐ   Titan is much larger than Saturn's other moons.

    Ⓑ   Saturn has over 60 moons orbiting it.

    Ⓒ   Saturn's largest moon is larger than Mercury.

    Ⓓ   Almost all of Saturn's moons have been named.

4   Which word does the author use to emphasize that Saturn has many moons?

    Ⓐ   *different*

    Ⓑ   *diverse*

    Ⓒ   *enormous*

    Ⓓ   *staggering*

Nintendo

Did you know that Nintendo didn't always make video game consoles? Before the first Nintendo gaming console was ever thought of, Nintendo was making playing cards!

Nintendo was originally founded in 1889 to make playing cards for a game called Hanafuda. Nintendo later tried many different business ideas before finding its niche. These included a taxi company, a television network, and a food company.

All of Nintendo's earlier business ventures failed. It was not until 1983 when Nintendo launched the original Nintendo Entertainment System (NES) that the company found commercial success. A handheld game console called the Game Boy followed in 1989.

The Nintendo DS and the Nintendo Wii were both highly successful.

It has since gone on to make other similar products. The Nintendo DS was released in 2004 and has sold over 150 million units. The Nintendo Wii was launched in 2006. It was a gaming system that was able to sense the movements of players, and use the physical movements of the player to direct the game. For example, someone playing tennis would swing the controller to cause the player in the game to swing the tennis racket. The Wii sold over 90 million units in less than 5 years.

CORE SKILLS PRACTICE

Which product represented the turning point for the company? Explain.

_____

_____

_____

_____

---

1   In the sentence below, which word could best replace <u>commercial</u>?

It was not until 1983 when Nintendo launched the original Nintendo Entertainment System (NES) that the company found commercial success.

Ⓐ   Business

Ⓑ   Long-term

Ⓒ   Significant

Ⓓ   Public

2   Why does the author begin the passage with a question?

Ⓐ   To get readers interested in the topic of the passage

Ⓑ   To show that the information may not be accurate

Ⓒ   To suggest that readers should research the topic

Ⓓ   To explain how Nintendo changed over the years

3   If the passage was given another title, which title would best fit?

Ⓐ   Collecting Playing Cards

Ⓑ   How to Play Nintendo

Ⓒ   The Beginnings of a Business

Ⓓ   The Future of Nintendo

4   What are the sales figures in the last paragraph used to show?

Ⓐ   Why Nintendo may eventually fail again

Ⓑ   How much each product cost

Ⓒ   Why people liked the products

Ⓓ   How successful each product was

Peace

Did you know that the peace symbol was originally created to protest against the use of nuclear weapons? It was designed by Gerald Holtom, a designer and graduate of London's Royal College of Arts, in 1958. He used the semaphore[1] letters for N and D to form the symbol. He chose those letters because they stood for nuclear disarmament. Holtom's design went on to become known worldwide as a general symbol for peace.

Semaphore Symbol for N   Semaphore Symbol for D   Peace Symbol

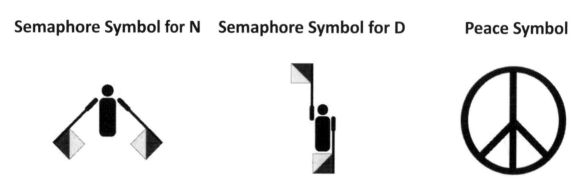

[1]Semaphore is a system of signaling that involves waving a pair of flags in a certain pattern. Each pattern represents a letter of the alphabet.

CORE SKILLS PRACTICE

How was the use of the peace symbol different from what Gerald Holtom expected? Explain your answer.

_____

_____

_____

_____

_____

1   What does the prefix in the word <u>disarmament</u> mean?

Ⓐ   Do the opposite of

Ⓑ   Two

Ⓒ   Before

Ⓓ   On the side of

2   What is the main purpose of the footnote?

Ⓐ   To define a term

Ⓑ   To state a reference

Ⓒ   To note a personal opinion

Ⓓ   To give a source

3   How do the diagrams mainly help the reader?

Ⓐ   They explain how symbols can represent complex ideas.

Ⓑ   They help show the purpose of using semaphore letters.

Ⓒ   They show how the semaphore letters combined to form the peace symbol.

Ⓓ   They indicate why the peace symbol was created.

4   Which conclusion is best supported by the information in the passage?

Ⓐ   The meaning of the peace symbol is only understood by a certain audience.

Ⓑ   The peace symbol today has a broader meaning than it initially did.

Ⓒ   The peace symbol is not used for the purpose it was intended for.

Ⓓ   The image of the peace symbol has been updated over the years.

Chess

Chess is a board game played on a checkerboard between two players. Each player has sixteen pieces. The goal is to use your pieces to trap or "checkmate" the king. A "checkmate" occurs when the king cannot move without being taken by another piece.

There are different rules for how each chess piece can move. For example, a rook can only move up or down, while a bishop can only move diagonally. The king can move in any direction, but can only move one space.

While it might seem simple, chess is a complex game. It takes a lot of strategy to win. Chess is about planning ahead. It is about considering what your opponent might do one, two, or many moves ahead. There are many different possibilities with every move, and it takes skill to consider them all and choose the best one.

Chess is thought to have originated from India or China, and is one of the oldest board games in existence. During the 16th century, it became popular as a competitive board game. The game has continued to grow since then. The first World Chess Champion was Wilhelm Steinitz, who claimed the title in 1886. In 2012, Viswanathan Anand (shown right) became the World Chess Champion for the fifth time. He first began playing chess at age 6.

© Marco Bonavoglia

CORE SKILLS PRACTICE

Use details from the passage to complete the table below.

Chess Piece	How It Can Move

---

1   In which paragraph does the author mainly give his personal views on chess?

Ⓐ   Paragraph 1

Ⓑ   Paragraph 2

Ⓒ   Paragraph 3

Ⓓ   Paragraph 4

2   Which word best describes the sentence below?

A "checkmate" occurs when the king cannot move without being taken by another piece.

Ⓐ   An exaggeration

Ⓑ   An instruction

Ⓒ   A definition

Ⓓ   An opinion

3   What is the main purpose of the third paragraph?

Ⓐ   To tell the challenges of chess

Ⓑ   To describe the history of chess

Ⓒ   To compare chess to other games

Ⓓ   To encourage people to play chess

4   The photograph of Viswanathan Anand best supports which idea?

Ⓐ   Chess skills require years of practice to develop.

Ⓑ   Chess has a long and interesting history.

Ⓒ   Chess games can take hours to complete.

Ⓓ   Chess takes a lot of concentration.

5   Many people have likened the game of chess to life. What do you think people can learn about life by playing chess? Use details from the passage to support your answer.

_____

_____

_____

_____

_____

_____

_____

_____

_____

_____

_____

_____

Reading Comprehension

Set 3

Literary and Informational Texts

Instructions

Read each passage. Complete the exercise under each passage.

Then complete the questions following each passage. For each multiple-choice question, fill in the circle for the correct answer. For other types of questions, follow the instructions given. Some of the questions require a written answer. Write your answer on the lines provided.

Monday

"Wow, that thing is annoying!" Kensi blurted out from her bed, as her hand slammed down on the alarm's snooze button.

"How on earth can it be six in the morning already?" she mumbled to herself.

After a long weekend of having fun with her friends, Kensi wasn't feeling anywhere near ready to start classes again. Kensi was slowly slipping away back to sleep when the alarm buzzed again.

BLARP, BLARP, BLARP!

Kensi jumped in shock. She buried her head into the pillow and pulled the blankets over her head, but there was no escape from the sound. She finally reached over and turned her alarm off, reluctantly getting out of bed. She stretched her arms and yawned.

"I really don't like Mondays!" Kensi muttered.

CORE SKILLS PRACTICE

The author suggests that Kensi is irritated by the alarm clock by describing her actions. Give **three** examples of actions that show Kensi's irritation.

1. _____

_____

2. _____

_____

3. _____

_____

1   In the sentence below, which word means about the same as <u>reluctantly</u>?

She finally reached over and turned her alarm off, reluctantly getting out of bed.

Ⓐ   Grumpily

Ⓑ   Finally

Ⓒ   Unwillingly

Ⓓ   Slowly

2   Why does the author most likely use upper case letters for the word "BLARP"?

Ⓐ   To indicate Kensi's feelings about the alarm clock

Ⓑ   To warn that Kensi will be in trouble if she sleeps in

Ⓒ   To show how many times the alarm clock buzzed

Ⓓ   To emphasize how loud the alarm clock was

3   What is Kensi's main problem in the passage?

Ⓐ   Her alarm clock is broken.

Ⓑ   She is going to be late for school.

Ⓒ   She does not want to wake up early.

Ⓓ   She had a bad night's sleep.

4   Why does Kensi ask the question in the second paragraph?

Ⓐ   She thinks she should not have to get up so early.

Ⓑ   She doesn't feel ready to get up yet.

Ⓒ   She wishes she had of gone to bed earlier.

Ⓓ   She guesses that her clock is set incorrectly.

Occam's Razor

Occam's razor is a useful and versatile scientific principle that scientists and others use to make decisions. It was developed by William of Ochkam in the 14th century. William of Ochkam was an English philosopher and friar. He produced many works on knowledge, logic, theology, and politics, but it is the principle named after him that he is remembered for.

The most useful interpretation is that if you have a number of competing theories that make the same prediction, the simpler one is usually better. This is sometimes simply stated as the idea that the simplest answer is often the correct one. Occam's razor is commonly applied in a wide range of scientific fields, from physics and mathematics to medicine.

What Happened?

When you wake up one day, there are puddles on your front lawn. The street in front of your house looks wet. You mention this over breakfast. Your mother says that it must have rained last night. Your younger brother says that the people across the road must have been filling their pool yesterday. They must have left the hose on all night and the street and your front lawn must have flooded.

It is *possible* that an overflowing pool caused the wet lawn and road. But the simplest answer is that it rained. It is most likely that it rained overnight.

CORE SKILLS PRACTICE

Give **one** example of a situation from everyday life where Occam's razor could be applied.

_____

_____

_____

---

1   Which word could best be used in place of <u>principle</u>?

Occam's razor is a useful and versatile scientific principle that scientists and others use to make decisions.

Ⓐ   Problem

Ⓑ   Theory

Ⓒ   Experiment

Ⓓ   Error

2   What is the main purpose of the passage?

Ⓐ   To instruct

Ⓑ   To entertain

Ⓒ   To inform

Ⓓ   To persuade

3   What is the main purpose of the information in the box?

Ⓐ   To explain that Occam's razor has many uses

Ⓑ   To give an example of applying Occam's razor

Ⓒ   To show that Occam's razor can be incorrect

Ⓓ   To explain how Occam's razor was developed

4   Which detail supports the idea that Occam's razor is versatile?

Ⓐ   It was developed in the 14th century.

Ⓑ   It is named after a friar and philosopher.

Ⓒ   It can be applied to a wide range of fields.

Ⓓ   Its creator produced works in many areas.

Beach Day

I love going to the beach! There aren't many things better to take your mind off the world than just lying around and doing not much of anything at all. You can wander along the edge of the ocean and enjoy the feel of your feet sinking into the cool sand. I sometimes stop to watch the rhythm of the waves as they roll in. And if you close your eyes, the sound of the waves breaking on the shore soothes your mind.

Whenever I'm relaxing at the beach, I lay there for hours and let my mind wander. All I need is a big old shady palm tree, a beach towel, a sandy beach, and some peace and quiet. It doesn't get much better than that! In fact, there is not a single place in the whole world that I would rather be!

CORE SKILLS PRACTICE

Describe how the photographs add to the meaning of the passage.

_____

_____

_____

_____

_____

_____

1 What does the phrase "let my mind wander" refer to?

Ⓐ   Daydreaming

Ⓑ   Planning

Ⓒ   Sleeping

Ⓓ   Hoping

2 What is the point of view in the passage?

Ⓐ   First person

Ⓑ   Second person

Ⓒ   Third person limited

Ⓓ   Third person omniscient

3 Why does the author most likely use exclamation marks in the passage?

Ⓐ   To create a sense of mystery

Ⓑ   To communicate her enthusiasm

Ⓒ   To indicate speech

Ⓓ   To emphasize how quiet it is

4 In which sentence from the passage does the author use hyperbole?

Ⓐ   "I love going to the beach!"

Ⓑ   "Whenever I'm relaxing at the beach, I lay there for hours and let my mind wander."

Ⓒ   "All I need is a big old shady palm tree, a beach towel, a sandy beach, and some peace and quiet."

Ⓓ   "In fact, there is not a single place in the whole world that I would rather be!"

Pigeons

Within the animal kingdom, Columbidae is the bird family consisting of species of doves and pigeons. Doves and pigeons are solid-bodied birds with short necks and short slender bills. Dove is generally the name given to the smaller birds within the family, while pigeons are usually larger. The species of the Columbidae family most people are familiar with is the rock pigeon or domestic pigeon. They are common in many cities throughout the world.

Rock pigeons once lived mainly on sea cliffs. However, they have adapted well to city life. They use buildings as a form of cliff, and are often seen on window ledges, on the tops of buildings, and on structures such as bridges. They often feed on food scraps and tend to congregate together in large groups. Pigeons are considered by many to be pests, especially in cities.

CORE SKILLS PRACTICE

The author states that rock pigeons "have adapted well to city life." Explain how the author supports this statement.

_____

_____

_____

_____

_____

1   Complete the chart below using information from the passage.

Appearance of Doves and Pigeons

Body	
Neck	
Bill	

2   What does the photograph best show?

Ⓐ   What pigeons living in cities eat

Ⓑ   How pigeons congregate together

Ⓒ   How city people feel about pigeons

Ⓓ   Where pigeons in cities nest

3   What is the main purpose of the passage?

Ⓐ   To give details about a type of bird

Ⓑ   To encourage people to feed pigeons

Ⓒ   To warn about the problems that pigeons cause

Ⓓ   To compare and contrast doves and pigeons

4   What does the word <u>congregate</u> mean in the sentence below?

They often feed on food scraps and tend to congregate together in large groups.

Ⓐ   Plan

Ⓑ   Gather

Ⓒ   Hunt

Ⓓ   Fly

5   Why do you think people in cities consider pigeons to be pests? Use information from the passage to support your answer.

_____

_____

_____

_____

_____

_____

_____

_____

_____

_____

_____

_____

_____

Reading Comprehension

Set 4

Literary and Informational Texts

Instructions

Read each passage. Complete the exercise under each passage.

Then complete the questions following each passage. For each multiple-choice question, fill in the circle for the correct answer. For other types of questions, follow the instructions given. Some of the questions require a written answer. Write your answer on the lines provided.

Bless You

Sneezing is a bodily reflex similar to a cough. It serves the same purpose of a cough, which is to remove foreign bodies and irritants from the body.

The scientific term for sneezing is sternutation. There are four main reasons that people sneeze.

- Irritation – people sneeze when something irritates the nose
- Light – people can sneeze when they are suddenly exposed to bright light
- Feeling full – some people have a rare condition where they sneeze as a response to feeling very full after a meal
- Infection – many infections by viruses, including the common cold, can cause people to sneeze

The most common reason people sneeze is due to irritation. Many people sneeze when they breathe in dust, pollen, or other irritants in the air. This condition is known as hay fever, and is most common in spring when there is a lot of pollen in the air.

CORE SKILLS PRACTICE

How is sneezing similar to coughing?

_____

_____

How is sneezing different from coughing?

_____

_____

1   How is the first paragraph mainly organized?

    Ⓐ   A problem is described and then a solution is given.

    Ⓑ   Events are described in the order they occur.

    Ⓒ   Facts are given to support an argument.

    Ⓓ   Two events are compared.

2   The illustration in the passage mainly relates to which cause of sneezing?

    Ⓐ   Pollen

    Ⓑ   Dust

    Ⓒ   Light

    Ⓓ   Viruses

3   According to the passage, which reason for sneezing is least common?

    Ⓐ   Irritation

    Ⓑ   Light

    Ⓒ   Feeling full

    Ⓓ   Infection

4   The first sentence of the second paragraph is best described as –

    Ⓐ   a comparison

    Ⓑ   a definition

    Ⓒ   an exaggeration

    Ⓓ   an assumption

Scorpion and Frog

 Once upon a time, a scorpion was slowly walking along a river bank. The scorpion was journeying north to find a log that he could use to cross to the other side. On his way, the scorpion saw a frog swimming by.

"Would you be so kind as to carry me across the river?" the scorpion called out to the frog. His question was met with silence, as the frog looked upon him with a distrustful expression. "My friend, I assure you that I will not sting you! For if I do, you will sink and I too shall drown," the scorpion said.

The frog thought for a moment and then nodded, moving closer to the river bank. The scorpion walked onto the frog's back and they began to make their way across the river. Halfway across the river, the frog felt a stinger lunge into its back. The frog began to feel weak and sank slowly into the current. The frog looked up at the scorpion.

"Why did you do that? Now you too will die!" the frog said. The scorpion looked down at the frog sadly. "I am sorry my new friend," he said. "I am a scorpion. It's my nature."

CORE SKILLS PRACTICE

What do you think is the message of the passage? Explain your answer.

_____

_____

_____

_____

_____

---

1   What type of passage is "Scorpion and Frog"?

   Ⓐ   Realistic fiction

   Ⓑ   Biography

   Ⓒ   Science fiction

   Ⓓ   Fable

2   Why does the frog most likely hesitate before agreeing to carry the scorpion across the river?

   Ⓐ   The frog thinks the scorpion can swim.

   Ⓑ   The frog doesn't want to go across the river.

   Ⓒ   The frog thinks the scorpion might be too heavy.

   Ⓓ   The frog worries that the scorpion might harm him.

3   What is the point of view in the passage?

   Ⓐ   First person

   Ⓑ   Second person

   Ⓒ   Third person limited

   Ⓓ   Third person omniscient

4   Which detail about the scorpion is least important in the passage?

   Ⓐ   He has a deadly sting.

   Ⓑ   He is traveling north.

   Ⓒ   He needs to cross the river.

   Ⓓ   He is unable to swim.

The Fox and the Hound

First published in 1967, *The Fox and the Hound* is a novel written by American novelist Daniel P. Mannix. The story follows the life of a red fox named Tod and his run-ins with Copper, a dog owned by a local hunter. During the year of its release, the novel was the winner of a number of literary awards.

Walt Disney Pictures eventually purchased the film rights to *The Fox and the Hound* and a film adaptation began production in 1977. The film cost about $12 million to make. At the time, it was the most expensive animated film ever made. It was released in 1981 and was very successful.

The film *The Fox and the Hound 2* was released in 2006. It was not as successful as the original. However, the story was still enchanting and entertaining.

CORE SKILLS PRACTICE

The author states that the film *The Fox and the Hound* was very successful. How could the author support this statement?

_____

_____

_____

_____

_____

_____

1   Based on the passage, which statement is most likely true?

Ⓐ   More expensive animated films have been made since *The Fox and the Hound*.

Ⓑ   *The Fox and the Hound 2* has been watched by more people than the original film.

Ⓒ   A third film will be released shortly.

Ⓓ   Daniel P. Mannix has written many novels that have been turned into films.

2   In which year was the film *The Fox and the Hound* released?

Ⓐ   1967

Ⓑ   1977

Ⓒ   1981

Ⓓ   2006

3   Which sentence from the passage contains an opinion?

Ⓐ   "First published in 1967, *The Fox and the Hound* is a novel written by American novelist Daniel P. Mannix."

Ⓑ   "The story follows the life of a red fox named Tod and his run-ins with Copper, a dog owned by a local hunter."

Ⓒ   "At the time, it was the most expensive animated film ever made."

Ⓓ   "However, the story was still enchanting and entertaining."

4   In the second paragraph, the word <u>adaptation</u> probably refers to –

Ⓐ   giving the novel a new title for the film

Ⓑ   adjusting the novel to suit a film

Ⓒ   developing new characters for the film

Ⓓ   creating a budget and plan for making the film

Disappearing Dessert

It was a windy autumn morning in the backstreets of Brooklyn, New York. Tony was walking to the barber shop carrying a brown paper bag filled with cannoli. Along the way, he stopped to talk with Vinnie at the newspaper stand and gave him a few cannolis. Tony said his goodbyes and continued on toward the barber shop.

Cannoli

©John Mueller

He had nearly arrived when he ran into Jen. The two spoke for a while and Tony gave Jen a handful of cannolis to eat for dessert that evening. Just around the corner from the barber shop, he saw Mr. Jackson walking his dog. He raced over to say hello, and then offered Mr. Jackson a cannoli. Tony kept walking, and finally made it to the barber shop.

"Uncle Benny! Here are the delicious cannolis you asked Mamma to make for you!" Tony exclaimed.

He handed over the brown paper bag to his Uncle Benny and left the shop to go back home. Uncle Benny looked into the bag to find nothing inside.

"Crazy boy, there are no cannolis in here," he grumbled. "He must have eaten them all on the way here. Well, I can't really blame him. They are awfully delicious."

CORE SKILLS PRACTICE

How does Uncle Benny feel about not getting any cannolis? Explain.

_____

_____

_____

1   Which detail from the passage best shows that Tony is generous?

Ⓐ   He stops to talk to everyone he knows.

Ⓑ   He offers to give everyone cannolis.

Ⓒ   Uncle Benny calls him a crazy boy.

Ⓓ   He bakes cannolis for his friends.

2   Who does Tony speak to first in the passage?

Ⓐ   Vinnie

Ⓑ   Jen

Ⓒ   Mr. Jackson

Ⓓ   Uncle Benny

3   What happened to the cannolis?

Ⓐ   Tony gave them away.

Ⓑ   They fell out of the bag.

Ⓒ   Mamma didn't put any in the bag.

Ⓓ   Tony ate them as he was walking.

4   What information does the photograph offer the reader?

Ⓐ   It shows how many cannolis Tony had.

Ⓑ   It shows why Uncle Benny asked for cannolis.

Ⓒ   It shows what a cannoli is.

Ⓓ   It shows what happened to the cannolis.

5   Do you think the passage is meant to be serious or humorous? Use information from the passage to support your answer.

_____

_____

_____

_____

_____

_____

_____

_____

_____

_____

_____

_____

_____

_____

_____

Reading Comprehension

Set 5

Paired Literary Texts

Instructions

This set contains a pair of passages. Read each passage on its own first. Complete the exercise under each passage. Then complete the questions following each passage.

For each multiple-choice question, fill in the circle for the correct answer. For other types of questions, follow the instructions given. Some of the questions require a written answer. Write your answer on the lines provided.

After reading both passages, you will answer one or more additional questions. You will use information from both passages to answer these questions. Write your answers on the lines provided.

The Cookie Thief

Max was sitting at his desk early one morning flipping wildly through the pages of his notebook and pinning up hastily written notes on his corkboard. Max had covered his entire corkboard with clues, and drawn maps of his house. He paced back and forth, stared at the board, and then remembered something else. He scribbled something on another piece of note paper and added it to the board. "I'm going to find out who ate my cookies if it's the last thing I do!" Max said as he worked away on his investigation. Max's dog Lucky just stared up at him.

Max jumped up and headed for his sister's room. Along with his father, she was the main suspect. Before he had even set foot outside of his room, Max tripped on something, stumbled, and fell. Max sat up and shook himself off. He looked around to see what he had tripped on. Right in front of him was a plastic bowl filled with cookie crumbs. Max suddenly remembered that he'd snuck out in the middle of the night for a snack. He was suddenly glad that he hadn't stormed in and blamed his sister.

CORE SKILLS PRACTICE

How does Max feel at the start of the passage?

_____

_____

_____

How does Max feel at the end of the passage?

_____

_____

_____

---

1   Read this statement from the passage.

I'm going to find out who ate my cookies if it's the last thing I do!

Which literary device does Max use in this statement?

Ⓐ   Symbolism, using an object to stand for something else

Ⓑ   Metaphor, comparing one object to another

Ⓒ   Personification, describing an object as if it has human qualities

Ⓓ   Hyperbole, using exaggeration to make a point

2   What happens right after Max sees the bowl of cookie crumbs?

Ⓐ   He trips over something.

Ⓑ   He decides that his sister is to blame.

Ⓒ   He remembers how he snacked the night before.

Ⓓ   He starts to investigate the missing cookies.

3   Who is responsible for the missing cookies?

Ⓐ   Max

Ⓑ   Lucky

Ⓒ   Max's father

Ⓓ   Max's sister

4   The image in the first sentence mainly shows that Max feels –

Ⓐ   determined

Ⓑ   baffled

Ⓒ   frantic

Ⓓ   guilty

Nana's Cookie Jar

I do love Nana's cookie jar.
The cookies are so enticing.
They're so chewy and so gooey.
Not like those pre-packed cookies
you can buy in any store.

Nana's choc chip cookies
have choc chips that are still warm and soft.
Then there are the ones
with the pink sticky icing!
Oh, don't forget the fruity ones,
And the fresh and fruity jam tarts!
Yep, I do love Nana's cookie jar.

CORE SKILLS PRACTICE

Explain how you can tell that the poem is written in free verse.

_____

_____

Identify the repetition in the poem.

_____

_____

Explain how the punctuation adds to the poem.

_____

_____

5   Which line from the poem contains rhyme?

　Ⓐ　"They're so chewy and so gooey."

　Ⓑ　"Nana's choc chip cookies"

　Ⓒ　"Oh, don't forget the fruity ones,"

　Ⓓ　"Yep, I do love Nana's cookie jar."

6   Based on the poem, how are Nana's cookies better than cookies from a store?

　Ⓐ　There are more to choose from.

　Ⓑ　They are better for you.

　Ⓒ　They are fresher.

　Ⓓ　They are cheaper.

7   The speaker's tone in the poem is best described as –

　Ⓐ　confident and hopeful

　Ⓑ　witty and comical

　Ⓒ　eager and impatient

　Ⓓ　positive and enthusiastic

8   In the second line, the word <u>enticing</u> means that the cookies are –

　Ⓐ　fresh

　Ⓑ　large

　Ⓒ　tasty

　Ⓓ　tempting

Directions: Use both passages to answer the following questions.

9   Both passages show a character's love for cookies. Contrast how the two passages communicate the main character's love for cookies. Use details from both passages to support your answer.

_____

_____

_____

_____

_____

_____

_____

_____

_____

_____

_____

_____

Reading Comprehension

Set 6

Paired Informational Texts

Instructions

This set contains a pair of passages. Read each passage on its own first. Complete the exercise under each passage. Then complete the questions following each passage.

For each multiple-choice question, fill in the circle for the correct answer. For other types of questions, follow the instructions given. Some of the questions require a written answer. Write your answer on the lines provided.

After reading both passages, you will answer one or more additional questions. You will use information from both passages to answer these questions. Write your answers on the lines provided.

Anne Frank

Anne Frank was a teenage girl who was given a diary for her thirteenth birthday. Anne used the diary to record the events she lived through during World War II. The diary describes her life from June 1942 until August 1944. During this time, Anne Frank and her family were living in hiding. The diary is a moving account of life during World War II. Despite the difficulty of Anne Frank's life, the diary is generally positive and uplifting.

The diary eventually found its way to a publisher in Amsterdam. The first edition of *The Diary of a Young Girl* was printed in 1947. It has since become one of the most widely read books in the world. It has been published in over 60 languages and read by over 10 million people worldwide.

"Everyone has inside of him a piece of good news. The good news is that you don't know how great you can be! How much you can love! What you can accomplish! And what your potential is!"

\- Anne Frank, *The Diary of a Young Girl*

CORE SKILLS PRACTICE

How does the quote relate to the passage? Explain your answer.

_____

_____

_____

_____

_____

1   Which meaning of the word <u>record</u> is used in the second sentence?

   Ⓐ   To indicate a measurement

   Ⓑ   To put something into lasting form

   Ⓒ   To copy sounds or images

   Ⓓ   To make a brief note

2   Which sentence from the passage contains an opinion?

   Ⓐ   "The diary describes her life from June 1942 until August 1944."

   Ⓑ   "The diary is a moving account of life during World War II."

   Ⓒ   "The first edition of *The Diary of a Young Girl* was printed in 1947."

   Ⓓ   "It has been published in over 60 languages and read by over 10 million people worldwide."

3   Which detail best supports the idea that *The Diary of a Young Girl* is one of the most widely read books in the world?

   Ⓐ   It was first printed in 1947.

   Ⓑ   It is set during World War II.

   Ⓒ   It has been published in 60 languages.

   Ⓓ   It is a moving book.

4   Which statement is most likely true about the author of the passage?

   Ⓐ   She admires Anne Frank's attitude.

   Ⓑ   She is curious about how the book was published.

   Ⓒ   She is surprised the book was so successful.

   Ⓓ   She feels sorry for Anne Frank and her family.

I Have a Dream

Martin Luther King, Jr. was born in 1929. He is one of the most famous people in history to be associated with the civil rights movement. At age 35, King became the youngest person to ever receive a Nobel Peace Prize. He received it for his tireless work to end racial inequality.

Martin Luther King gave his famous speech to a crowd of over 200,000.

He is probably best known for his "I Have a Dream" speech. He delivered this famous speech after leading the 1963 March on Washington. Martin Luther King is honored with his own holiday. The third Monday of January every year is Martin Luther King, Jr. Day.

"I have a dream that my four children will one day live in a nation where they will not be judged by the color of their skin but by the content of their character."

-1963, Martin Luther King, Jr.

CORE SKILLS PRACTICE

What is the message of the quote from Martin Luther King's speech?

_____

_____

_____

_____

---

5 In the first paragraph, which word means about the same as <u>tireless</u>?

Ⓐ Difficult

Ⓑ Effective

Ⓒ Essential

Ⓓ Determined

6 What type of passage is "I Have a Dream"?

Ⓐ Biography

Ⓑ Short story

Ⓒ Autobiography

Ⓓ News article

7 Which sentence from the passage best supports the idea that the work of Martin Luther King, Jr. is appreciated?

Ⓐ "Martin Luther King, Jr. was born in 1929."

Ⓑ "He is probably best known for his 'I Have a Dream' speech."

Ⓒ "He delivered this famous speech after leading the 1963 March on Washington."

Ⓓ "Martin Luther King is honored with his own holiday."

8 What does the photograph most help readers understand?

Ⓐ How moving King's speech was

Ⓑ Why King felt his speech was important

Ⓒ How many people gathered to listen to King's speech

Ⓓ The impact that King's speech had on the fight for equality

Directions: Use both passages to answer the following question.

9   How do both passages show that people's words can inspire others? Use
details from both passages to support your answer.

_____

_____

_____

_____

_____

_____

_____

_____

_____

_____

_____

_____

_____

Reading Comprehension

Set 7

Literary Texts

Instructions

Read each passage. Complete the exercise under each passage.

Then complete the questions following each passage. For each multiple-choice question, fill in the circle for the correct answer. For other types of questions, follow the instructions given. Some of the questions require a written answer. Write your answer on the lines provided.

Musical Tastes

February 22

Dear Diary,

Today after school, I went over to Megan's house. We finished our homework, and then we talked about school and music. Megan is really into those really loud bands that seem to scream all the words. I just don't get it! Why listen to music if you can't even understand the words? Give me something I can sing to any day! Megan wanted me to listen to some songs. She turned on her CD player really loud. Suddenly it was like the room was filled with screaming monkeys. I listened to a few songs and really tried to enjoy it, but it just wasn't my thing. I guess we'll have to agree to disagree about music!

Bye for now,

Holly

CORE SKILLS PRACTICE

In the passage, Holly describes how she has different tastes in music than her friend Megan. Do you think friends need to have similar tastes and interests?

_____

_____

_____

_____

_____

---

1   Holly writes that "I just don't get it!" What does Holly mean by this?

ⓐ   I don't understand.

ⓑ   I don't own any music.

ⓒ   I don't want to listen to it.

ⓓ   I don't enjoy it at all.

2   Which literary device is used in the sentence below?

Suddenly it was like the room was filled with screaming monkeys.

ⓐ   Simile

ⓑ   Metaphor

ⓒ   Alliteration

ⓓ   Symbolism

3   What can the reader tell because the passage has a first-person point of view?

ⓐ   Why Holly went to Megan's house

ⓑ   How Holly felt about Megan's music

ⓒ   What Megan's music sounded like

ⓓ   What Holly did at Megan's house

4   The dis in disagree means the same as the dis in –

ⓐ   dishonest

ⓑ   distance

ⓒ   disaster

ⓓ   discussion

Dreams of Gold

Saturday had always been the day Marcy went to swimming class. Ever since she was six years old, Marcy and her mother had gone to the local swim center to practice with Coach Tyler and all of the other children from her neighborhood. Marcy loved swimming and had always been faster than everybody else in her class. Almost every night, Marcy dreamed about winning a gold medal at the state swimming competition.

Then a girl called Morgan joined the class. Morgan swam faster than anyone Marcy had ever seen. Her legs kicked at a rapid pace and her arms were a blur of movement. Suddenly, Marcy wasn't the fastest swimmer anymore.

CORE SKILLS PRACTICE

You can make predictions by using information in a passage as well as your own prior knowledge and ideas. Answer the question below by making a prediction.

How do you think Marcy feels when Morgan joins the swimming class?

_____

_____

_____

_____

_____

_____

1   Why does the author most likely describe Morgan's arms as a "blur of movement"?

Ⓐ   To tell how her arms were mainly underwater

Ⓑ   To explain that Marcy felt jealous of Morgan

Ⓒ   To show that she did not have the correct style

Ⓓ   To emphasize how fast her arms moved

2   Who is the main character in the passage?

Ⓐ   Marcy

Ⓑ   Marcy's mother

Ⓒ   Coach Tyler

Ⓓ   Morgan

3   How is the title of the passage relevant?

Ⓐ   It describes what Marcy wants.

Ⓑ   It shows that swimming is enjoyable.

Ⓒ   It suggests that Morgan will defeat Marcy.

Ⓓ   It refers to the challenge that Marcy must overcome.

4   In which sentence does <u>center</u> mean the same as in the first paragraph?

Ⓐ   Mrs. Harper's children are the <u>center</u> of her world.

Ⓑ   To make a paper airplane, first fold the paper down the <u>center</u>.

Ⓒ   The arts <u>center</u> offers classes in drawing, painting, and sculpture.

Ⓓ   I thought the pie was ready, but the <u>center</u> was still cold.

Mindful of Monsters

When you find yourself alone at night do you fathom, wonder about, or ponder on the idea of monsters under your bed? Perhaps you think the possibility is ridiculous. Because monsters don't exist, right? Well, that is what I would want you to think if I were a monster.

I guess you never bother to check under your bed, in your closet, or behind all those closed doors anymore. Maybe there is a monster lurking somewhere you no longer look. Maybe it's time to check. Or, if the monster has never bothered you before, maybe you just leave him alone to hide quietly in his home.

CORE SKILLS PRACTICE

Do you think the author of the passage really believes that there are monsters hiding somewhere? Explain why or why not.

_____

_____

_____

_____

_____

_____

_____

_____

1   Which word means about the same as <u>ridiculous</u>?

    Ⓐ   Ordinary

    Ⓑ   Silly

    Ⓒ   Rare

    Ⓓ   Special

2   Which word best describes the tone of the passage?

    Ⓐ   Curious

    Ⓑ   Creepy

    Ⓒ   Serious

    Ⓓ   Playful

3   What is the most likely reason the author asks questions in the passage?

    Ⓐ   To communicate the author's uncertainty

    Ⓑ   To engage and interest the reader

    Ⓒ   To suggest that readers should research the topic

    Ⓓ   To show that the passage is fiction

4   Why does the author most likely choose the word <u>lurking</u> instead of <u>hiding</u>?

    Ⓐ   To make the monster seem sneaky

    Ⓑ   To add humor to the passage

    Ⓒ   To show that monsters move quietly

    Ⓓ   To suggest that monsters need not be feared

Missing a Friend

Lying underneath a star-sprinkled sky,
Here I ponder just wondering why,
For it was this day years ago we met,
I miss you now, my dear faithful pet.

CORE SKILLS PRACTICE

The poet uses carefully-chosen words and phrases to help communicate meaning in the poem. Describe the purpose of each word or phrase listed below.

star-sprinkled sky: _____

_____

_____

ponder: _____

_____

_____

dear faithful pet: _____

_____

_____

1   How would the poet most likely sound if she was reading the poem aloud?

    Ⓐ   Somber

    Ⓑ   Mysterious

    Ⓒ   Frustrated

    Ⓓ   Cheerful

2   Which literary device is used in the first line of the poem?

    Ⓐ   Alliteration

    Ⓑ   Repetition

    Ⓒ   Simile

    Ⓓ   Personification

3   What is the rhyme pattern of the poem?

    Ⓐ   Every line rhymes.

    Ⓑ   The second and fourth lines rhyme.

    Ⓒ   The first and last lines rhyme.

    Ⓓ   There are two sets of rhyming lines.

4   The poet is most likely thinking about the pet because –

    Ⓐ   she thinks about the pet every evening

    Ⓑ   it is the anniversary of the day she first got the pet

    Ⓒ   she is considering getting another pet

    Ⓓ   it is the first night she will be without her pet

5 Explain how you can tell that the poet cares about her pet. Use information from the passage to support your answer.

_____

_____

_____

_____

_____

_____

_____

_____

_____

_____

_____

_____

_____

_____

Reading Comprehension

Set 8

Informational Texts

Instructions

Read each passage. Complete the exercise under each passage.

Then complete the questions following each passage. For each multiple-choice question, fill in the circle for the correct answer. For other types of questions, follow the instructions given. Some of the questions require a written answer. Write your answer on the lines provided.

Albertosaurus

The albertosaurus was a carnivorous dinosaur that lived around 65 million years ago. The albertosaurus was discovered after fossils were found in Alberta, Canada in 1884. The dinosaurs were thought to live only in North America.

The albertosaurus was similar to its famous relative the tyrannosaurus, but was much smaller in size. Albertosaurus dinosaurs are thought to have weighed less than 2 ton and to have grown to around 30 feet. The tyrannosaurus could weigh around 7 ton and could grow to just over 40 feet.

The albertosaurus looked similar to the tyrannosaurus.
While it is still larger than a person and would certainly
be a scary sight, it's nowhere near as awe-inspiring as
the massive tyrannosaurus.

CORE SKILLS PRACTICE

Why do you think the albertosaurus is not as well-known as the tyrannosaurus?

_____

_____

_____

_____

_____

1 According to the passage, what is the main difference between the albertosaurus and the tyrannosaurus?

Ⓐ   When it lived

Ⓑ   What it ate

Ⓒ   How large it was

Ⓓ   Where it lived

2 You can infer from the passage that the albertosaurus was named after –

Ⓐ   the person who discovered the dinosaur's fossils

Ⓑ   where the dinosaur's fossils were discovered

Ⓒ   what the dinosaur ate

Ⓓ   what the dinosaur looked like

3 If the author wanted to show the size difference between the albertosaurus and other dinosaurs, which of these could NOT be used?

Ⓐ   Chart

Ⓑ   Graph

Ⓒ   Illustration

Ⓓ   Timeline

4 The word <u>carnivorous</u> refers to –

Ⓐ   what the dinosaur ate

Ⓑ   where the dinosaur lived

Ⓒ   how long ago the dinosaur lived

Ⓓ   the size of the dinosaur

Doyle Brunson

Affectionately known as "Big Poppa" or "Texas Dolly," Doyle Brunson is one of the most respected professional card players in the world. He is easily recognized in his trademark cowboy hat. He has been playing cards professionally for over 50 years.

Brunson was born in 1933 in Fisher County, Texas. He is one of only three players ever to win back to back main event titles at the World Series of Poker. He won these titles in 1976 and 1977. He has gone on to achieve many other great things, but nothing quite as amazing as this pair of championship wins.

The two wins of 1976 and 1977 have gone down in history for another reason. Each time he won, Brunson was holding the same two cards in the final hand. They were a ten and a two. It was a coincidence that stunned everybody at the time, and is still remembered today. In fact, this hand is now known by card players everywhere as "The Brunson."

CORE SKILLS PRACTICE

You can often guess how authors feel about a topic by what they say and what words they use. How do you think the author feels about Doyle Brunson?

_____

_____

_____

_____

_____

---

1 The author states that Brunson "is one of only three players ever to win back to back main event titles." What does the phrase "back to back" show about the wins?

    Ⓐ   They were both easy wins.

    Ⓑ   They occurred one after the other.

    Ⓒ   They happened against the same opponent.

    Ⓓ   They both required a lot of hard work.

2 Which sentence best supports the idea that Doyle Brunson is a successful professional card player?

    Ⓐ   "He is easily recognized in his trademark cowboy hat."

    Ⓑ   "Brunson was born in 1933 in Fisher County, Texas."

    Ⓒ   "He is one of only three players ever to win back to back main event titles at the World Series of Poker."

    Ⓓ   "Each time he won, Brunson was holding the same two cards in the final hand."

3 Which word best describes the tone of the passage?

    Ⓐ   Admiring

    Ⓑ   Objective

    Ⓒ   Lively

    Ⓓ   Sentimental

4 In the last paragraph, why does the author use the word stunned?

    Ⓐ   To suggest that Brunson was very lucky

    Ⓑ   To emphasize how surprised everyone was

    Ⓒ   To show that some people passed out

    Ⓓ   To explain that there were great celebrations

Food Poisoning

Bacteria grow quickly in the right conditions. When food isn't prepared, kept, or handled properly it has the potential to make you very ill. Food poisoning occurs when bacteria are introduced into food before it is eaten. Luckily, it is quite easy to prevent food poisoning. All you have to do is follow a few simple rules.

1: Wash your hands and the equipment you're going to use to prepare and serve the food.

2: Don't use the same chopping board for chopping meat that you use to prepare fruit and vegetables.

3: Ensure your food is cooked thoroughly. The cooking process destroys most harmful bacteria, so this step can prevent food poisoning even when the raw food contains bacteria.

4: Properly store your food.

5: Make sure your refrigerator temperature is set low enough.

6: Follow the directions on packaging for how to store foods once they are open, and for how long to store food for.

7: Don't unfreeze and then refreeze food.

Top Tip
Many foods have to be used in a few days once they are open. It's easy to forget when a food was opened. Keep a marker near the fridge and write on the packet what date the food was opened.

CORE SKILLS PRACTICE

The author states that food poisoning can make you very ill. Describe how the author could add more specific information to make this point clearer.

_____

_____

_____

1   In rule 3, which word could best be used in place of <u>thoroughly</u>?

    Ⓐ   Quickly

    Ⓑ   Completely

    Ⓒ   Cleanly

    Ⓓ   Nicely

2   Which rule does the information in the box mainly relate to?

    Ⓐ   Rule 4

    Ⓑ   Rule 5

    Ⓒ   Rule 6

    Ⓓ   Rule 7

3   What is the main purpose of the first paragraph?

    Ⓐ   To describe how to prevent food poisoning

    Ⓑ   To explain the importance of food safety

    Ⓒ   To encourage people to cook their own food

    Ⓓ   To show that bacteria can grow anywhere

4   Which rule from the passage supports the conclusion that bacteria grow poorly in cold conditions?

    Ⓐ   "Don't use the same chopping board for chopping meat that you use to prepare fruit and vegetables."

    Ⓑ   "Ensure your food is cooked thoroughly."

    Ⓒ   "Make sure your refrigerator temperature is set low enough."

    Ⓓ   "Don't unfreeze and then refreeze food."

Computer Health

Many of us receive vaccinations and booster shots from time to time to keep us healthy and help stop the spread of viruses. Computers are much the same! We should all make sure a quality antivirus program is installed and updated frequently on our home computers. How should we do this?

Step 1: Research what antivirus software you think would be best to use.

Step 2: Install it onto your computer and update the virus definition database.

Step 3: Run a scan of your computer to make sure your drive is free from viruses.

Step 4: Keep updating the software often to make sure it can spot new viruses.

TIP

New viruses are being created all the time. A virus program can only fight the viruses it knows about. That's why it is important to update your virus program often. Every time you update the software, it will be told about new viruses. It is a good idea to set a day each week to check that your software is up-to-date.

CORE SKILLS PRACTICE

Why does the author compare a person getting a booster shot to a computer having an antivirus program?

_____

_____

_____

_____

1   Which two words from the passage have about the same meaning?

    Ⓐ   Healthy, virus

    Ⓑ   Installed, updated

    Ⓒ   Frequently, often

    Ⓓ   Computers, software

2   What is the main purpose of the passage?

    Ⓐ   To describe what an antivirus program is

    Ⓑ   To encourage people to protect their computers

    Ⓒ   To explain how computers are similar to people

    Ⓓ   To show that viruses can damage computers

3   What is the information in the box mostly about?

    Ⓐ   Choosing your software

    Ⓑ   Updating your software

    Ⓒ   Buying your software

    Ⓓ   Cleaning your software

4   Which statement is most relevant to the passage?

    Ⓐ   The best things in life are free.

    Ⓑ   Many hands make light work.

    Ⓒ   Prevention is better than cure.

    Ⓓ   Actions speak louder than words.

5   Do you think it is important to have an up-to-date antivirus program on
your computer? Use details from the passage to support your answer.

_____

_____

_____

_____

_____

_____

_____

_____

_____

_____

_____

_____

_____

_____

Reading Comprehension

Set 9

Literary and Informational Texts

Instructions

Read each passage. Complete the exercise under each passage.

Then complete the questions following each passage. For each multiple-choice question, fill in the circle for the correct answer. For other types of questions, follow the instructions given. Some of the questions require a written answer. Write your answer on the lines provided.

First Day

The siren blared and all of the officers started running around the locker room.

"Woop! Woop! Emergency call. Corner of George and Main. Woop! Woop!" came over the loudspeaker.

It was Chris's first day on the job and he was noticeably anxious.

"Suit up, Rookie. We've got you every step of the way!" Sergeant Carter yelled as he was pulling on his vest.

Chris nodded and finished gearing up, feeling a little more confident he could get through his first day.

CORE SKILLS PRACTICE

Think about what would happen next in the story. Write a paragraph or two that continues the story.

_____

_____

_____

_____

_____

_____

_____

1   Read this sentence from the passage.

We've got you every step of the way!

Which statement best summarizes the meaning of this sentence?

Ⓐ   We'll carry you upstairs.

Ⓑ   We'll look after and support you.

Ⓒ   We'll be watching you closely.

Ⓓ   We'll be in charge of you.

2   It is most likely Chris's first day as a —

Ⓐ   doctor

Ⓑ   firefighter

Ⓒ   security guard

Ⓓ   park ranger

3   Which word best describes Sergeant Carter?

Ⓐ   Encouraging

Ⓑ   Demanding

Ⓒ   Nervous

Ⓓ   Insensitive

4   The author uses the word <u>blared</u> in the first sentence to suggest that the siren was —

Ⓐ   high-pitched

Ⓑ   muffled

Ⓒ   unexpected

Ⓓ   piercing

Amelia Earhart

Born in 1897, Amelia Earhart is an American aviation pioneer. She was the first woman to fly solo across the Atlantic Ocean. At that time, it was rare for females to be pilots, let alone be record-breaking pilots! Earhart set many other aviation records during her life, and also wrote about her experiences. She became a celebrity in the United States, and appeared in many advertisements.

The Purdue University funded an ill-fated flight of the globe in 1937. Sadly, Amelia Earhart and her navigator disappeared over the central Pacific Ocean. To this day, it is unknown what actually happened. Some researchers believe that the plane crashed into the ocean and sank. Another theory is that Amelia landed at an uninhabited island called Gardner Island. There have been many other theories, but none have ever been proven. It may never be known what happened to Amelia Earhart. However, she can still always be remembered as a great pilot who achieved many incredible things.

CORE SKILLS PRACTICE

Do you think Amelia Earhart's solo flight would be as significant if it occurred today? Explain why or why not.

_____

_____

_____

_____

_____

1   What does the word <u>ill-fated</u> suggest about the flight funded by Purdue University?

    Ⓐ   It cost too much.

    Ⓑ   It ended badly.

    Ⓒ   It was poorly planned.

    Ⓓ   It did not take place.

2   Why did Amelia Earhart have to fight hard to achieve her dream?

    Ⓐ   Flying was quite new and people feared it was unsafe.

    Ⓑ   People worried that she would have an accident.

    Ⓒ   She was more interested in being famous than training.

    Ⓓ   Many people did not think that women could be pilots at the time.

3   Amelia Earhart was the first woman to fly solo across which ocean?

    Ⓐ   Atlantic Ocean

    Ⓑ   Pacific Ocean

    Ⓒ   Arctic Ocean

    Ⓓ   Indian Ocean

4   Which sentence best supports the idea that Earhart gained recognition for her achievements?

    Ⓐ   "She was the first woman to fly solo across the Atlantic Ocean."

    Ⓑ   "She became a celebrity in the United States, and appeared in many advertisements."

    Ⓒ   "Sadly, Amelia Earhart and her navigator disappeared over the central Pacific Ocean."

    Ⓓ   "It may never be known what happened to Amelia Earhart."

Poor King Henri

As the snow began to fall over the Halls of Alloric, King Henri became grumpy and quite bothersome to his loyal subjects. King Henri never meant to be a bother. He never meant to be so abrupt or abrasive. He did enjoy the company of his friends and fellows. It was just that all this cold made Henri's knee ache and throb constantly. It was the aching that he could not bear. He thought about the aching all day, and often snapped at the people around him. He tossed and turned all night, becoming more and more tired by the day. As the days became colder, King Henri's friends began to avoid him. He was often left alone, where he thought about his aching joints even more. By the end of winter, he was eating alone every night.

Then the spring would come and everything would change. King Henri would emerge from his grumpy loneliness like a flower blooming in the warmth of the spring sunshine. King Henri marked the occasion by throwing a large celebration. For days, a fabulous feast and festival would go on. All this was to thank everyone for being so understanding of his peculiar ways.

CORE SKILLS PRACTICE

Do you think King Henri's friends would be understanding of his changes of mood? Use details from the passage to support your answer.

_____

_____

_____

_____

_____

---

1   Which sentence best explains why King Henri throws a large celebration every year?

    Ⓐ   "He did enjoy the company of his friends and fellows."

    Ⓑ   "It was just that all this cold made Henri's knee ache and throb constantly."

    Ⓒ   "For days, a fabulous feast and festival would go on."

    Ⓓ   "All this was to thank everyone for being so understanding of his peculiar ways."

2   Which of these is the main clue to the past setting of the passage?

    Ⓐ   The events in the passage occur during a cold winter.

    Ⓑ   The main event at the end of a passage is a celebration.

    Ⓒ   The main character in the passage suffers from aching knees.

    Ⓓ   The passage is about a king and his subjects.

3   Which set of words from the passage is an example of alliteration?

    Ⓐ   "snow began to fall"

    Ⓑ   "company of his friends"

    Ⓒ   "ache and throb constantly"

    Ⓓ   "fabulous feast and festival"

4   The word <u>abrasive</u> describes how King Henri is –

    Ⓐ   uncomfortable

    Ⓑ   rude

    Ⓒ   impatient

    Ⓓ   selfish

The students in Jack's class were asked to write a short essay about an inspirational person from their town. Jack wrote this essay about Dr. Price.

A Helping Hand

Dr. Price is always trying to help different people in different parts of the world. Recently, he flew to Japan to help the local doctors and aid teams after a large earthquake shook their country. The year before, he traveled to Africa to provide healthcare to people living in poverty. Each year, he travels to schools all over America and talks to students about healthcare issues. He does all this without getting paid for it.

Dr. Price is a wealthy and successful doctor in our town, and his services are always in demand. But he never forgets how important it is to help people less fortunate. Dr. Price has always believed that many people taking small steps can make a big difference. We may not all be able to do what Dr. Price does, but we can all learn from his example and find a way to help others.

CORE SKILLS PRACTICE

List **three** examples that Jack gives of Dr. Price helping people.

1. _____

_____

2. _____

_____

3. _____

_____

---

1   Jack's main purpose in the passage was probably to –

   Ⓐ   encourage people to become doctors

   Ⓑ   describe the life of Dr. Price

   Ⓒ   inspire people to try to make a difference

   Ⓓ   explain to readers why Dr. Price is often away

2   What does Jack most admire about Dr. Price?

   Ⓐ   How he is a successful doctor

   Ⓑ   How he travels the world

   Ⓒ   How he helps others

   Ⓓ   How he is wealthy

3   Which word best describes Dr. Price?

   Ⓐ   Charitable

   Ⓑ   Adventurous

   Ⓒ   Determined

   Ⓓ   Optimistic

4   What does the title of the passage most likely refer to?

   Ⓐ   How doctors use their hands to heal

   Ⓑ   How Dr. Price wants to help people

   Ⓒ   How not all people have access to healthcare

   Ⓓ   How many people are needed when disasters occur

5 Do you think Dr. Price is an inspirational person? Use information from the passage to support your answer.

_____

_____

_____

_____

_____

_____

_____

_____

_____

_____

_____

_____

_____

Reading Comprehension

Set 10

Literary and Informational Texts

Instructions

Read each passage. Complete the exercise under each passage.

Then complete the questions following each passage. For each multiple-choice question, fill in the circle for the correct answer. For other types of questions, follow the instructions given. Some of the questions require a written answer. Write your answer on the lines provided.

Tau Ceti

Tau Ceti is a large star located within the Cetus constellation. It is similar to our Sun in both mass and spectral type. It is located just under 12 light years from our Solar System, and can be seen by the naked eye. In astronomy, that's a very close star. It has been the focus of extensive searches for extraterrestrial life. It is thought to have five planets orbiting it and one of them could be quite similar to Earth, and similar enough to support life.

In 2004, Jane Greaves and her team of astronomers discovered that Tau Ceti has almost 10 times more debris orbiting it than our own Sun. This means that the planet would be impacted by meteors quite often. Due to this debris, the possibility of finding evidence of life surrounding the star is very unlikely. However, Tau Ceti is still often used in science fiction books and films as a solar system found to have life.

CORE SKILLS PRACTICE

The word *extraterrestrial* is made by adding the prefix *extra-* to the word *terrestrial*. The word prefix *extra-* means "outside or beyond" and the word *terrestrial* means "relating to the Earth." Complete the table below by adding the meaning of each word to the table.

Word	Meaning
extraterrestrial	outside of the Earth
extracurricular	
extraordinary	
extrasensory	

---

1   What does the word <u>extensive</u> mean in the passage?

    Ⓐ   Complex

    Ⓑ   Costly

    Ⓒ   Widespread

    Ⓓ   Unsuccessful

2   What is the main difference between Tau Ceti and the Sun?

    Ⓐ   Its mass

    Ⓑ   Its spectral type

    Ⓒ   Whether it can be seen with the naked eye

    Ⓓ   How much debris orbits it

3   What is the main purpose of the second paragraph?

    Ⓐ   To show that Tau Ceti probably does not have a planet with life

    Ⓑ   To give background information about how Tau Ceti was discovered

    Ⓒ   To explain how scientists study stars that are relatively close to Earth

    Ⓓ   To illustrate that the star needs to be studied further

4   Which prediction is best supported by the information in the passage?

    Ⓐ   It is unlikely that there is a planet with life orbiting Tau Ceti.

    Ⓑ   Jane Greaves still believes that Tau Ceti is home to a form of life.

    Ⓒ   The debris surrounding Tau Ceti has been studied for signs of life.

    Ⓓ   Scientists have accepted that there is no other life in the universe.

The Exam

March 6

Dear Annie,

I hope you are well. I'm a little worried about failing my math exam this week. I can do the geometry pretty easily. For some reason, shapes just make sense to me. But a lot of the algebra problems just look like strings of numbers, symbols, and funky letters. It's like a tapestry of symbols that my brain just can't understand.

As you know, my brother Kevin is quite a whiz at math. I asked him for some help, but he's not very good at explaining things simply. In fact, he really just confused me even more! Mom is going to help me study and is also going to ask if Miss Bert will help tutor me during lunch tomorrow. That would definitely be helpful. I'll let you know how I go in my next letter.

Bye for now,

Alex

CORE SKILLS PRACTICE

Alex refers to algebra as being "like a tapestry of symbols." Do you think this is a good description?

_____

_____

_____

_____

1   Why does the author use the word <u>whiz</u> in the sentence below?

   As you know, my brother Kevin is quite a whiz at math.

   Ⓐ   To show that Kevin is very busy

   Ⓑ   To show that Kevin is good at math

   Ⓒ   To show that Kevin works quickly

   Ⓓ   To show that Kevin makes a hissing sound

2   Complete the web with **three** things that Alex does to try to learn algebra.

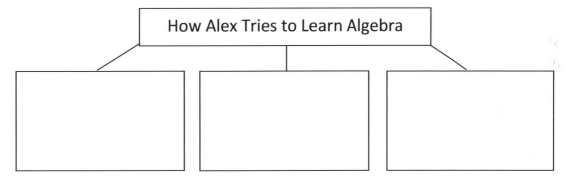

3   Which word would Alex use to describe the algebra problems?

   Ⓐ   Confusing

   Ⓑ   Simple

   Ⓒ   Fascinating

   Ⓓ   Tedious

4   How is the letter mainly organized?

   Ⓐ   Alex describes a problem and then tells the solution.

   Ⓑ   Alex compares how he feels now with how he will feel later.

   Ⓒ   Alex describes current events and then predicts future events.

   Ⓓ   Alex gives facts about his studies and then gives opinions.

Constantinople

The Fall of Constantinople occurred thousands of years ago. The historical event was an important turning point in history. It involved the capture of the capital of the Byzantine Empire by the Ottomans. This event took place in 1453. Before this, the Byzantine Empire had seemed unstoppable. It had been the most powerful and wealthiest empire in Europe for over five hundred years.

The Fall of Constantinople marked the end of Emperor Constantine XI's rule. It was also the end of the Byzantine Empire. After the conquest, Constantinople became the Ottoman Empire's new capital.

CORE SKILLS PRACTICE

Imagine that you want to write a report about what life was like in the city of Constantinople in the 1400s. Write a list of questions you could research and answer in your report.

1. _____

2. _____

3. _____

4. _____

1   What does the "Fall of Constantinople" refer to?

    Ⓐ   How the city of Constantinople was destroyed

    Ⓑ   How people fled from the city of Constantinople

    Ⓒ   How the city of Constantinople was divided in two

    Ⓓ   How the city of Constantinople was taken over

2   Which sentence from the passage contains an opinion?

    Ⓐ   "The Fall of Constantinople occurred thousands of years ago."

    Ⓑ   "Before this, the Byzantine Empire had seemed unstoppable."

    Ⓒ   "The Fall of Constantinople marked the end of Emperor Constantine XI's rule."

    Ⓓ   "After the conquest, Constantinople became the Ottoman Empire's new capital."

3   Where would this passage most likely be found?

    Ⓐ   In a book of poems

    Ⓑ   In an encyclopedia

    Ⓒ   In a science textbook

    Ⓓ   In a book of short stories

4   If the passage were given another title, which title would best fit?

    Ⓐ   The Rise of the Byzantine Empire

    Ⓑ   A City to Remember

    Ⓒ   A Turning Point in History

    Ⓓ   How to Accept Change

Going to a Show

It was summer holidays. For Jacob, that meant going home to Lakewater. He wouldn't usually be so excited about it, but this summer was different. This summer, he was going to be seeing Dodger in concert.

Jacob had won four free tickets to see his favorite band after uploading a video of him singing one of their songs to an online contest. Seeing Dodger would be something Jacob would never forget.

The biggest problem he'd had was trying to choose just three friends to take with him. He wished that all his friends could go. He had finally chosen the three friends that he knew adored Dodger just as much as he did. He felt sad about not taking his best friend Andrew, but he knew that Andrew didn't like Dodger's music that much. Jacob's friends were all overjoyed when he told them the good news. Now the concert was just a week away and Jacob could hardly wait.

CORE SKILLS PRACTICE

Explain why Jacob probably had mixed feelings about winning the free tickets at first. In your answer, describe why he would have felt both good and bad about it.

_____

_____

_____

_____

_____

_____

1   Which word means the opposite of <u>adored</u>?

   (A)   Loved

   (B)   Despised

   (C)   Copied

   (D)   Understood

2   The passage is most like –

   (A)   an essay

   (B)   an advertisement

   (C)   a short story

   (D)   a news article

3   What is the point of view of the passage?

   (A)   First person

   (B)   Second person

   (C)   Third person limited

   (D)   Third person omniscient

4   What is Jacob's main problem in the passage?

   (A)   He is unsure who to take to the concert with him.

   (B)   He does not want to ever forget the concert.

   (C)   He has to wait too long for the concert.

   (D)   He won free tickets to a concert.

5 Do you think the way Jacob chose which friends to take was fair? Explain why or why not.

_____

_____

_____

_____

_____

_____

_____

_____

_____

_____

_____

_____

_____

Reading Comprehension

Set 11

Paired Literary Texts

Instructions

This set contains a pair of passages. Read each passage on its own first. Complete the exercise under each passage. Then complete the questions following each passage.

For each multiple-choice question, fill in the circle for the correct answer. For other types of questions, follow the instructions given. Some of the questions require a written answer. Write your answer on the lines provided.

After reading both passages, you will answer one or more additional questions. You will use information from both passages to answer these questions. Write your answers on the lines provided.

The Old Hollow Bakery

Peering through the window at Old Hollow Bakery, you could see a selection of fine treats. There would be wonderful brownies, mouth-watering cakes, fresh cookies, and a large assortment of other goodies.

It was all in a day's work for Mrs. Dunn, the baker from Old Hollow. Mrs. Dunn loved opening her shop in the morning. All the town's children would rush in on their way to school and pick themselves up some tasty treats.

Mrs. Dunn didn't even mind getting up so early. When she got up, the sun hadn't even peeked its head above the horizon. As she baked, the sun slowly rose. Finally, it was time for the children to arrive. They rushed in to see what treats she had made for them. Just one smile made Mrs. Dunn feel like all the hard work was worth it.

CORE SKILLS PRACTICE

How does the author show that the bakery is popular?

_____

_____

_____

How does the author show that Mrs. Dunn is a good baker?

_____

_____

_____

---

1   Which meaning of the word <u>fine</u> is used in the first sentence?

Ⓐ   Not coarse

Ⓑ   Sunny or clear

Ⓒ   Very thin

Ⓓ   Good

2   Which literary device is used in the sentence below?

When she got up, the sun hadn't even peeked its head above the horizon.

Ⓐ   Personification

Ⓑ   Simile

Ⓒ   Metaphor

Ⓓ   Symbolism

3   Which word best describes Mrs. Dunn?

Ⓐ   Lazy

Ⓑ   Creative

Ⓒ   Giving

Ⓓ   Smart

4   The details about Mrs. Dunn getting up so early are probably included to –

Ⓐ   make readers feel sorry for her

Ⓑ   show how dedicated she is

Ⓒ   suggest that the customers do not appreciate her

Ⓓ   explain why the town's children often stop in

The Highest Price

The bell chimed at the entry door to the Captain's quarters. "Come," Captain Ludikar beckoned. The door slid open and in walked Commander Sever. "Captain, just checking if you're okay," Sever said with concern in his voice. Ludikar smirked and turned toward Sever.

"We may have lost a lot of good people today. Am I okay? Yes. I'm okay because I'm still here. The problem is I don't know if they're okay. They're down there on that planet, our mission failed today, and now we can't pick them up until morning. That is what's bothering me," Captain Ludikar replied.

"They're well-trained, well-prepared, and I feel sure they will survive the night. Meanwhile, we're preparing to go in and pick them up at first light tomorrow. Rest easy, Captain, I know we have this under control," Commander Sever replied.

Captain Ludikar nodded and tried to smile, but he knew he would be getting little sleep until he knew that his people were safe.

CORE SKILLS PRACTICE

Read Captain Ludikar's dialogue in paragraph 2. How would Captain Ludikar most likely sound?

_____

_____

_____

_____

_____

5   This passage is told from the point of view of —

Ⓐ   Commander Sever

Ⓑ   Captain Ludikar

Ⓒ   one of the men on the planet

Ⓓ   a person outside the story

6   The passage is most like —

Ⓐ   science fiction

Ⓑ   historical fiction

Ⓒ   a mystery

Ⓓ   a fable

7   What does the title of the passage most likely refer to?

Ⓐ   The amount of money the mission cost

Ⓑ   The possible consequences of the mission failure

Ⓒ   The way that Captain Ludikar feels about failing

Ⓓ   The determination that Commander Sever feels

8   Which word best describes Commander Sever?

Ⓐ   Energetic

Ⓑ   Arrogant

Ⓒ   Confident

Ⓓ   Anxious

Directions: Use both passages to answer the following question.

9   Even though Captain Ludikar and Mrs. Dunn have very different jobs, they both have similar motivations. Explain how their motivations are similar. Use details from both passages to support your answer.

_____

_____

_____

_____

_____

_____

_____

_____

_____

_____

_____

_____

_____

_____

Reading Comprehension

Set 12

Paired Informational Texts

Instructions

This set contains a pair of passages. Read each passage on its own first. Complete the exercise under each passage. Then complete the questions following each passage.

For each multiple-choice question, fill in the circle for the correct answer. For other types of questions, follow the instructions given. Some of the questions require a written answer. Write your answer on the lines provided.

After reading both passages, you will answer one or more additional questions. You will use information from both passages to answer these questions. Write your answers on the lines provided.

The Ambassadors

The oil painting titled *The Ambassadors* was created by Hans Holbein the Younger in 1533. Hans Holbein the Younger was a German artist best known for painting portraits. The painting is a portrait of two people, and also contains a number of carefully drawn items. It has been the subject of much discussion through art studies and literature.

The Ambassadors is most famous for the introduction of anamorphic design into hand-painted art. Anamorphic design refers to design where images can only be seen from a certain angle. At the bottom of *The Ambassadors*, a skewed object can be seen. From front on, you cannot tell what the object is. If you are viewing the painting from the side, the same object is easily recognizable as a skull.

The strange object at the bottom of the painting looks like a skull when viewed from the side.

The painting can be viewed in Great Britain's National Gallery, which is located in London. While the painting may not immediately seem interesting, it is definitely worth a second look.

CORE SKILLS PRACTICE

Explain how *The Ambassadors* is an example of anamorphic design.

_____

_____

_____

_____

1   Based on the passage, which detail about *The Ambassadors* makes it most interesting?

    Ⓐ   That it is an oil painting

    Ⓑ   That it was painted in 1533

    Ⓒ   That it is a portrait of two people

    Ⓓ   That it contains anamorphic design

2   Where was Hans Holbein from?

    Ⓐ   Holland

    Ⓑ   Germany

    Ⓒ   Great Britain

    Ⓓ   United States

3   Which sentence from the passage gives the author's opinion?

    Ⓐ   "The oil painting titled *The Ambassadors* was created by Hans Holbein the Younger in 1533."

    Ⓑ   "At the bottom of *The Ambassadors*, a skewed object can be seen."

    Ⓒ   "The painting can be viewed in Great Britain's National Gallery, which is located in London."

    Ⓓ   "While the painting may not immediately seem interesting, it is definitely worth a second look."

4   Which word could best be used in place of skewed?

    Ⓐ   Distorted

    Ⓑ   Magical

    Ⓒ   Unknown

    Ⓓ   Puzzling

Michelangelo

Born in 1475, Michelangelo was a genius of both academics and artistry. He lived during the Renaissance, which was a time in Europe when art was thriving. He was considered a typical Renaissance man. This term refers to people with talents in many different areas. While he is best known as an artist and sculptor, he was also a poet, an engineer, and an architect.

Michelangelo's work became renowned pieces of the period in which he lived. The statue of *David*, completed in 1504, is arguably one of Michelangelo's most famous works. It was sculpted from marble, and took over two years to complete.

A close-up view of the statue of *David* shows the striking detail of the sculpture.

A less known fact about the statue is that it was originally intended to be placed on the roof of the Florence Cathedral. Just before it was complete, people realized that placing it on the Florence Cathedral would be impossible. The statue weighed over 6 ton. While the roof would probably be able to support the weight, it would have been almost impossible to lift the statue to put it up there. This was in the 1500s before cranes and other machinery would have made the task a lot simpler! The statue was placed in a public square in Florence instead. It can be found today at the Academy of Fine Arts in Florence. Visitors to Florence can also see a replica of the famous statue where it was originally placed.

CORE SKILLS PRACTICE

How did the time period affect the problem described in the last paragraph?

_____

_____

_____

---

5   What does the close-up view of the statue best help readers understand?

Ⓐ   Why the statue was so heavy

Ⓑ   Why the statue lasted so long

Ⓒ   Why the statue took so long to complete

Ⓓ   Why the statue was placed in a public square

6   In the first paragraph, the word <u>thriving</u> shows that art was —

Ⓐ   costly

Ⓑ   varied

Ⓒ   disliked

Ⓓ   popular

7   Which sentence best supports the idea that Michelangelo was a "typical Renaissance man"?

Ⓐ   "This term refers to people with talents in many different areas."

Ⓑ   "While he is best known as an artist and sculptor, he was also a poet, an engineer, and an architect."

Ⓒ   "Michelangelo's work became renowned pieces of the period in which he lived."

Ⓓ   "The statue of *David*, completed in 1504, is arguably one of Michelangelo's most famous works."

8   What is the main purpose of the last paragraph?

Ⓐ   To explain that the statue on the Florence Cathedral isn't real

Ⓑ   To give an interesting anecdote about the statue

Ⓒ   To describe what made Michelangelo's work so impressive

Ⓓ   To show how skilled Michelangelo was for the time in which he lived

Directions: Use both passages to answer the following question.

9   Compare what makes *The Ambassadors* and the statue of *David* special. In your answer, explain how details play a role in making both artworks special. Use details from both passages to support your answer.

_____

_____

_____

_____

_____

_____

_____

_____

_____

_____

_____

_____

_____

ANSWER KEY

Common Core State Standards

The state of New Jersey has adopted the Common Core State Standards. These standards describe what students are expected to know. Student learning throughout the year is based on these standards, and all the questions on the state tests assess these standards.

All the exercises and questions in this book cover the Common Core State Standards. This book will develop all the Common Core reading skills, as well as complementary writing and language skills.

Core Skills Practice

Each passage includes an exercise focused on one key skill described in the Common Core standards. The answer key identifies the core skill covered by each exercise, and describes what to look for in the student's response.

Common Core Reading Standards

The Common Core reading standards are divided into the following two areas:

- Reading Standards for Literature
- Reading Standards for Informational Text

Within each of these areas, there are nine standards that describe specific skills the student should have. The answer key on the following pages lists the standard assessed by each question. The skill listed can be used to identify a student's areas of strength and weakness, so revision and instruction can be targeted accordingly.

Scoring Constructed-Response Questions

This workbook includes constructed-response questions, where students provide a written answer to a question. The answer key gives guidance on how to score these questions. Use the criteria listed as a guide to scoring these questions, and as a guide for giving the student advice on how to improve an answer.

Set 1: Literary Texts

Not a Farmer's Day

Core Skills Practice

Core skill: Analyze how particular elements of a story or drama interact.

Answer: The student should explain that Noah forgets to set the brakes on his tractor because he is so tired from building the chicken coop. The student should explain that forgetting to put the brakes on causes the chicken coop to be destroyed.

Question	Answer	Common Core Reading Standard
1	B	Determine the meaning of words and phrases as they are used in a text, including figurative and connotative meanings.
2	B	Analyze how particular elements of a story or drama interact.
3	C	Cite several pieces of textual evidence to support analysis of what the text says explicitly as well as inferences drawn from the text.
4	C	Determine a theme or central idea of a text and analyze its development over the course of the text; provide an objective summary of the text.

The Violet

Core Skills Practice

Core skill: Determine the meaning of words and phrases as they are used in a text, including figurative and connotative meanings.

Answer: The student should list the adjectives modest, lovely, and pretty. The student should explain that all three adjectives show the positive aspects and beauty of the flower.

Question	Answer	Common Core Reading Standard
1	A	Analyze how an author develops and contrasts the points of view of different characters or narrators in a text.
2	B	Analyze the impact of rhymes and other repetitions of sounds (e.g., alliteration) on a specific verse or stanza of a poem or section of a story or drama.
3	B	Determine a theme or central idea of a text and analyze its development over the course of the text; provide an objective summary of the text.
4	C	Analyze the impact of rhymes and other repetitions of sounds (e.g., alliteration) on a specific verse or stanza of a poem or section of a story or drama.

A Challenge

Core Skills Practice

Core skill: Cite several pieces of textual evidence to support analysis of what the text says explicitly as well as inferences drawn from the text.

Answer: The student should make a reasonable inference about how Reggie feels about being unable to solve the Rubik's Cube. The inference could be that Reggie feels challenged, frustrated, or determined. The answer should include support from the passage, such as how he says he just can't solve it, how he says he's been trying for months, or how he ends by saying he will try again tomorrow.

Question	Answer	Common Core Reading Standard
1	C	Determine the meaning of words and phrases as they are used in a text, including figurative and connotative meanings.
2	C	Cite several pieces of textual evidence to support analysis of what the text says explicitly as well as inferences drawn from the text.
3	A	Compare and contrast a written story, drama, or poem to its audio, filmed, staged, or multimedia version, analyzing the effects of techniques unique to each medium.
4	A	Analyze how an author develops and contrasts the points of view of different characters or narrators in a text.

The New Boy

Core Skills Practice

Core skill: Determine a theme or central idea of a text and analyze its development over the course of the text; provide an objective summary of the text.

Answer: The student should write a short summary of the story. The summary should include the main events from the story.

Question	Answer	Common Core Reading Standard
1	C	Determine the meaning of words and phrases as they are used in a text, including figurative and connotative meanings.
2	D	Determine a theme or central idea of a text and analyze its development over the course of the text; provide an objective summary of the text.
3	C	Cite several pieces of textual evidence to support analysis of what the text says explicitly as well as inferences drawn from the text.
4	B	Analyze how particular elements of a story or drama interact.
5	See Below	Determine a theme or central idea of a text and analyze its development over the course of the text; provide an objective summary of the text.

Give a score of 0, 1, 2, 3, or 4 based on how well the answer meets the criteria listed.
- It should explain the message the passage has about judging people.
- It should refer to how the new boy is judged on his unusual appearance, and how Lionel's mother says that Lionel won't know what the boy is like until he gives him a chance.
- It should use relevant details from the passage.
- It should be well-organized, clear, and easy to understand.

Set 2: Informational Texts

Many Moons

Core Skills Practice

Core skill: Compare and contrast a text to an audio, video, or multimedia version of the text, analyzing each medium's portrayal of the subject.

Answer: The student should describe a diagram that shows the relative sizes of Titan, Mercury, and the Earth's moon. The student may refer to showing the relative size of each body, or labeling each body with its size.

Question	Answer	Common Core Reading Standard
1	B	Determine the meaning of words and phrases as they are used in a text, including figurative, connotative, and technical meanings.
2	C	Analyze the structure an author uses to organize a text, including how the major sections contribute to the whole and to the development of the ideas.
3	A	Trace and evaluate the argument and specific claims in a text, assessing whether the reasoning is sound and the evidence is relevant and sufficient to support the claims.
4	D	Analyze the impact of a specific word choice on meaning and tone.

Nintendo

Core Skills Practice

Core skill: Analyze the interactions between individuals, events, and ideas in a text.

Answer: The student should identify that the Nintendo Entertainment System (NES) represented the turning point for the company because it was the product that first made the company successful.

Question	Answer	Common Core Reading Standard
1	A	Determine the meaning of words and phrases as they are used in a text, including figurative, connotative, and technical meanings.
2	A	Analyze the structure an author uses to organize a text, including how the major sections contribute to the whole and to the development of the ideas.
3	C	Determine two or more central ideas in a text and analyze their development over the course of the text; provide an objective summary of the text.
4	D	Trace and evaluate the argument and specific claims in a text, assessing whether the reasoning is sound and the evidence is relevant and sufficient to support the claims.

Peace

Core Skills Practice

Core skill: Determine two or more central ideas in a text and analyze their development over the course of the text; provide an objective summary of the text.

Answer: The student should explain that the peace symbol became more widely used than Gerald Holtom expected, or was used to stand for peace in general instead of only nuclear disarmament.

Question	Answer	Common Core Reading Standard
1	A	Determine the meaning of words and phrases as they are used in a text, including figurative, connotative, and technical meanings.
2	A	Analyze the structure an author uses to organize a text, including how the major sections contribute to the whole and to the development of the ideas.
3	C	Compare and contrast a text to an audio, video, or multimedia version of the text, analyzing each medium's portrayal of the subject.
4	B	Determine two or more central ideas in a text and analyze their development over the course of the text; provide an objective summary of the text.

Chess

Core Skills Practice

Core skill: Cite several pieces of textual evidence to support analysis of what the text says explicitly as well as inferences drawn from the text.

Answer: The student should complete the table as follows:

rook   up or down
bishop   diagonally
king   one space in any direction

Question	Answer	Common Core Reading Standard
1	C	Determine an author's point of view or purpose in a text and analyze how the author distinguishes his or her position from that of others.
2	C	Analyze the structure an author uses to organize a text, including how the major sections contribute to the whole and to the development of the ideas.
3	A	Determine two or more central ideas in a text and analyze their development over the course of the text; provide an objective summary of the text.
4	D	Compare and contrast a text to an audio, video, or multimedia version of the text, analyzing each medium's portrayal of the subject.
5	See Below	Analyze the interactions between individuals, events, and ideas in a text.

Give a score of 0, 1, 2, 3, or 4 based on how well the answer meets the criteria listed.
- It should describe what people can learn about life from chess.
- It should relate the challenges and processes of chess to those in life.
- It may refer to how chess is about planning ahead, predicting what other people will do, and choosing from many different possibilities.
- It should be well-organized, clear, and easy to understand.

Set 3: Literary and Informational Texts

Monday

Core Skills Practice

Core skill: Analyze how an author develops and contrasts the points of view of different characters or narrators in a text.

Answer: The student should give two examples that show Kensi's irritation. Examples include how Kensi jumps when the alarm goes off, how Kensi buries her head into the pillow, how Kensi pulls the blanket over her head, or how Kensi says that she does not like Mondays.

Question	Answer	Common Core Reading Standard
1	C	Determine the meaning of words and phrases as they are used in a text, including figurative and connotative meanings.
2	D	Analyze how a drama's or poem's form or structure contributes to its meaning.
3	C	Determine a theme or central idea of a text and analyze its development over the course of the text; provide an objective summary of the text.
4	B	Cite several pieces of textual evidence to support analysis of what the text says explicitly as well as inferences drawn from the text.

Occam's Razor

Core Skills Practice

Core skill: Analyze the interactions between individuals, events, and ideas in a text.

Answer: The student should give an example from everyday life of how Occam's razor could be applied. The example should be a situation where the simplest answer is the correct one.

Question	Answer	Common Core Reading Standard
1	B	Determine the meaning of words and phrases as they are used in a text, including figurative, connotative, and technical meanings.
2	C	Determine an author's point of view or purpose in a text and analyze how the author distinguishes his or her position from that of others.
3	B	Determine two or more central ideas in a text and analyze their development over the course of the text; provide an objective summary of the text.
4	C	Trace and evaluate the argument and specific claims in a text, assessing whether the reasoning is sound and the evidence is relevant and sufficient to support the claims.

Beach Day

Core Skills Practice

Core skill: Compare and contrast a written story, drama, or poem to its audio, filmed, staged, or multimedia version, analyzing the effects of techniques unique to each medium.

Answer: The student should give a reasonable description of how the photographs add to the meaning. The answer could refer to how they suggest things the speaker does at the beach, how they help show that the beach is a relaxing place, or how they help the reader imagine the sights and sounds of the beach.

Question	Answer	Common Core Reading Standard
1	A	Determine the meaning of words and phrases as they are used in a text, including figurative and connotative meanings.
2	A	Analyze how an author develops and contrasts the points of view of different characters or narrators in a text.
3	B	Analyze how a drama's or poem's form or structure contributes to its meaning.
4	D	Determine the meaning of words and phrases as they are used in a text, including figurative and connotative meanings.

Pigeons

Core Skills Practice

Core skill: Trace and evaluate the argument and specific claims in a text, assessing whether the reasoning is sound and the evidence is relevant and sufficient to support the claims.

Answer: The student should describe how the author shows that rock pigeons have adapted well to city life. The answer should refer to how they use buildings as if they are cliffs.

Question	Answer	Common Core Reading Standard
1	Solid Short Short, slender	Cite several pieces of textual evidence to support analysis of what the text says explicitly as well as inferences drawn from the text.
2	B	Compare and contrast a text to an audio, video, or multimedia version of the text, analyzing each medium's portrayal of the subject.
3	A	Determine an author's point of view or purpose in a text and analyze how the author distinguishes his or her position from that of others.
4	B	Determine the meaning of words and phrases as they are used in a text, including figurative, connotative, and technical meanings.
5	See Below	Analyze the interactions between individuals, events, and ideas in a text.

Give a score of 0, 1, 2, 3, or 4 based on how well the answer meets the criteria listed.

- It should make reasonable inferences about why people in cities consider pigeons to be pests.
- The reasons may include that pigeons congregate together, that they are noisy, that they make a mess, or that they look unappealing.
- It should use relevant details from the passage, and may also use prior knowledge and personal opinion.
- It should be well-organized, clear, and easy to understand.

Set 4: Literary and Informational Texts

Bless You

Core Skills Practice

Core skill: Analyze the interactions between individuals, events, and ideas in a text.

Answer: The student should describe one similarity between coughing and sneezing, such as that they both have the purpose of removing foreign bodies from the body. The student should describe one difference between coughing and sneezing, such as that sneezing is more violent than coughing.

Question	Answer	Common Core Reading Standard
1	D	Analyze the structure an author uses to organize a text, including how the major sections contribute to the whole and to the development of the ideas.
2	A	Compare and contrast a text to an audio, video, or multimedia version of the text, analyzing each medium's portrayal of the subject.
3	C	Cite several pieces of textual evidence to support analysis of what the text says explicitly as well as inferences drawn from the text.
4	B	Analyze the structure an author uses to organize a text, including how the major sections contribute to the whole and to the development of the ideas.

Scorpion and Frog

Core Skills Practice

Core skill: Determine a theme or central idea of a text and analyze its development over the course of the text; provide an objective summary of the text.

Answer: The student should identify the theme as being about people not being able to change who they are, or about not being too trusting of others.

Question	Answer	Common Core Reading Standard
1	D	Analyze how a drama's or poem's form or structure contributes to its meaning.
2	D	Cite several pieces of textual evidence to support analysis of what the text says explicitly as well as inferences drawn from the text.
3	D	Analyze how an author develops and contrasts the points of view of different characters or narrators in a text.
4	B	Analyze how particular elements of a story or drama interact.

The Fox and the Hound

Core Skills Practice

Core skill: Trace and evaluate the argument and specific claims in a text, assessing whether the reasoning is sound and the evidence is relevant and sufficient to support the claims.

Answer: The student should identify relevant details that could be added to show that the film was successful. Possible relevant details include facts on how much money the film made, facts about how many people saw the film, and details about awards the film received.

Question	Answer	Common Core Reading Standard
1	A	Cite several pieces of textual evidence to support analysis of what the text says explicitly as well as inferences drawn from the text.
2	C	Cite several pieces of textual evidence to support analysis of what the text says explicitly as well as inferences drawn from the text.
3	D	Trace and evaluate the argument and specific claims in a text, assessing whether the reasoning is sound and the evidence is relevant and sufficient to support the claims.
4	B	Determine the meaning of words and phrases as they are used in a text, including figurative, connotative, and technical meanings.

Disappearing Dessert

Core Skills Practice

Core skill: Cite several pieces of textual evidence to support analysis of what the text says explicitly as well as inferences drawn from the text.

Answer: The student should make a reasonable inference about how Uncle Benny feels. The student could infer that he is disappointed based on how he says how delicious they are, or could infer that he is understanding based on how he says that he doesn't blame Tony for eating them.

Question	Answer	Common Core Reading Standard
1	B	Cite several pieces of textual evidence to support analysis of what the text says explicitly as well as inferences drawn from the text.
2	A	Determine a theme or central idea of a text and analyze its development over the course of the text; provide an objective summary of the text.
3	A	Analyze how particular elements of a story or drama interact.
4	C	Compare and contrast a written story, drama, or poem to its audio, filmed, staged, or multimedia version, analyzing the effects of techniques unique to each medium.
5	See Below	Analyze how a drama's or poem's form or structure contributes to its meaning.

Give a score of 0, 1, 2, 3, or 4 based on how well the answer meets the criteria listed.
- It should identify that the passage is meant to be humorous.
- It should include a fully-supported explanation of how you can tell that the passage is meant to be humorous.
- It should use relevant details from the passage.
- It should be well-organized, clear, and easy to understand.

Set 5: Paired Literary Texts

The Cookie Thief/Nana's Cookie Jar

Core Skills Practice

Core skill:	Analyze how particular elements of a story or drama interact.
Answer:	The student should describe how Max feels upset, annoyed, or determined at the start of the passage. The student should describe how Max feels relieved, embarrassed, or amused at the end of the passage.

Core Skills Practice

Core skill:	Analyze how a drama's or poem's form or structure contributes to its meaning.
Answer:	The student should explain that the poem is free verse because it lacks any set structure in its rhyme or rhythm. The student should identify the repetition of "I do love Nana's cookie jar" in the first and last lines of the poem. The student may describe how the exclamation marks add to how positive and upbeat the poem is, or may describe how the punctuation makes the poem seem conversational.

Question	Answer	Common Core Reading Standard
1	D	Determine the meaning of words and phrases as they are used in a text, including figurative and connotative meanings.
2	C	Determine a theme or central idea of a text and analyze its development over the course of the text; provide an objective summary of the text.
3	A	Cite several pieces of textual evidence to support analysis of what the text says explicitly as well as inferences drawn from the text.
4	C	Analyze how an author develops and contrasts the points of view of different characters or narrators in a text.
5	A	Analyze the impact of rhymes and other repetitions of sounds (e.g., alliteration) on a specific verse or stanza of a poem or section of a story or drama.
6	C	Cite several pieces of textual evidence to support analysis of what the text says explicitly as well as inferences drawn from the text.
7	D	Analyze how an author develops and contrasts the points of view of different characters or narrators in a text.
8	D	Determine the meaning of words and phrases as they are used in a text, including figurative and connotative meanings.
9	See Below	Determine a theme or central idea of a text and analyze its development over the course of the text; provide an objective summary of the text.

Give a score of 0, 1, 2, 3, or 4 based on how well the answer meets the criteria listed.

- It should give a reasonable comparison of how the two passages show the character's love for cookies.
- It should show an understanding that the love for cookies is stated directly in the poem, while Max's love for cookies is shown through his actions and by how upset he is when he thinks someone has eaten his cookies.
- It should use relevant details from both passages.
- It should be well-organized, clear, and easy to understand.

Set 6: Paired Informational Texts

Anne Frank/I Have a Dream

Core Skills Practice

Core skill: Compare and contrast a text to an audio, video, or multimedia version of the text, analyzing each medium's portrayal of the subject.

Answer: The student should describe the connection between the content of the passage and the quote. The student may describe how the quote is from the book described in the passage. The student may also describe how the quote shows how the book is positive and uplifting.

Core Skills Practice

Core skill: Determine two or more central ideas in a text and analyze their development over the course of the text; provide an objective summary of the text.

Answer: The student should explain that the message of the speech is that everyone should be treated equally, or that people should not be judged based on their skin color.

Question	Answer	Common Core Reading Standard
1	B	Determine the meaning of words and phrases as they are used in a text, including figurative, connotative, and technical meanings.
2	B	Trace and evaluate the argument and specific claims in a text, assessing whether the reasoning is sound and the evidence is relevant and sufficient to support the claims.
3	C	Cite several pieces of textual evidence to support analysis of what the text says explicitly as well as inferences drawn from the text.
4	A	Determine an author's point of view or purpose in a text and analyze how the author distinguishes his or her position from that of others.
5	D	Determine the meaning of words and phrases as they are used in a text, including figurative, connotative, and technical meanings.
6	A	Analyze the structure an author uses to organize a text, including how the major sections contribute to the whole and to the development of the ideas.
7	D	Cite several pieces of textual evidence to support analysis of what the text says explicitly as well as inferences drawn from the text.
8	C	Compare and contrast a text to an audio, video, or multimedia version of the text, analyzing each medium's portrayal of the subject.
9	See Below	Analyze how two or more authors writing about the same topic shape their presentations of key information by emphasizing different evidence or advancing different interpretations of facts.

Give a score of 0, 1, 2, 3, or 4 based on how well the answer meets the criteria listed.
- It should give a reasonable analysis of how both passages show that people's words can inspire others.
- It may refer to how both passages show the impact of one person's words and to how both passages include an example of the person's inspiring words.
- It should use relevant details from both passages.
- It should be well-organized, clear, and easy to understand.

Set 7: Literary Texts

Musical Tastes

Core Skills Practice

Core skill: Cite several pieces of textual evidence to support analysis of what the text says explicitly as well as inferences drawn from the text.

Answer: The student should draw a conclusion about whether friends need to have similar tastes and interests. The answer may refer to how Holly shows that you can still get along with a friend who has different tastes from you, or may refer to how Holly and Megan will never be able to enjoy listening to music together.

Question	Answer	Common Core Reading Standard
1	A	Cite several pieces of textual evidence to support analysis of what the text says explicitly as well as inferences drawn from the text.
2	A	Determine the meaning of words and phrases as they are used in a text, including figurative and connotative meanings.
3	B	Analyze how an author develops and contrasts the points of view of different characters or narrators in a text.
4	A	Determine the meaning of words and phrases as they are used in a text, including figurative and connotative meanings.

Dreams of Gold

Core Skills Practice

Core skill: Analyze how particular elements of a story or drama interact.

Answer: The student should make a valid prediction about how Marcy feels when Morgan joins the swimming class. The prediction could be that Marcy feels jealous, upset, challenged, or inspired. Any reasonable prediction is acceptable as long as it is supported and explained. Students should use prior knowledge and their own ideas in their answer.

Question	Answer	Common Core Reading Standard
1	D	Determine the meaning of words and phrases as they are used in a text, including figurative and connotative meanings.
2	A	Analyze how particular elements of a story or drama interact.
3	A	Analyze how a drama's or poem's form or structure contributes to its meaning.
4	C	Determine the meaning of words and phrases as they are used in a text, including figurative and connotative meanings.

Mindful of Monsters

Core Skills Practice

Core skill: Analyze how an author develops and contrasts the points of view of different characters or narrators in a text.

Answer: The student should explain whether or not the author really believes that there are monsters hiding somewhere. Students should indicate that the author does not really believe in monsters, and should show an understanding that the author wrote the passage to entertain rather than give a serious warning.

Question	Answer	Common Core Reading Standard
1	B	Determine the meaning of words and phrases as they are used in a text, including figurative and connotative meanings.
2	D	Analyze how an author develops and contrasts the points of view of different characters or narrators in a text.
3	B	Analyze how a drama's or poem's form or structure contributes to its meaning.
4	A	Determine the meaning of words and phrases as they are used in a text, including figurative and connotative meanings.

Missing a Friend

Core Skills Practice

Core skill: Determine the meaning of words and phrases as they are used in a text, including figurative and connotative meanings.

Answer: The student should give a reasonable description of the purpose of each word or phrase. The student could describe the literal meaning of each, but could also refer to the effect of each word or phrase on the reader. Examples are given below.

 star-sprinkled sky: This phrase creates an image of the night sky. The alliteration also creates a sense of stillness.

 ponder: The word shows that the speaker is thinking about her pet. The word *ponder* also creates a sense of sadness.

 dear faithful pet: This phrase makes the pet seem special and shows how much the speaker cares about the pet.

Question	Answer	Common Core Reading Standard
1	A	Compare and contrast a written story, drama, or poem to its audio, filmed, staged, or multimedia version, analyzing the effects of techniques unique to each medium.
2	A	Analyze the impact of rhymes and other repetitions of sounds (e.g., alliteration) on a specific verse or stanza of a poem or section of a story or drama.
3	D	Analyze the impact of rhymes and other repetitions of sounds (e.g., alliteration) on a specific verse or stanza of a poem or section of a story or drama.
4	B	Analyze how particular elements of a story or drama interact.
5	See Below	Cite several pieces of textual evidence to support analysis of what the text says explicitly as well as inferences drawn from the text.

Give a score of 0, 1, 2, 3, or 4 based on how well the answer meets the criteria listed.

- It should provide a fully-supported explanation of how you can tell that the poet cares about her pet.
- The details may include that the poet is thinking about her pet, that the poet misses her pet, or that the poet refers to her pet as "my dear faithful pet."
- It should use relevant details from the poem.
- It should be well-organized, clear, and easy to understand.

Set 8: Informational Texts

Albertosaurus

Core Skills Practice

Core skill: Cite several pieces of textual evidence to support analysis of what the text says explicitly as well as inferences drawn from the text.

Answer: The student should give an opinion on why the albertosaurus is not as well-known as the tyrannosaurus. The answer should refer to how it was smaller than the tyrannosaurus and does not seem as fearsome.

Question	Answer	Common Core Reading Standard
1	C	Analyze the interactions between individuals, events, and ideas in a text.
2	B	Cite several pieces of textual evidence to support analysis of what the text says explicitly as well as inferences drawn from the text.
3	D	Compare and contrast a text to an audio, video, or multimedia version of the text, analyzing each medium's portrayal of the subject.
4	A	Determine the meaning of words and phrases as they are used in a text, including figurative, connotative, and technical meanings.

Doyle Brunson

Core Skills Practice

Core skill: Determine an author's point of view or purpose in a text and analyze how the author distinguishes his or her position from that of others.

Answer: The student should make an inference about how the author feels about Doyle Brunson. The inference could be that the author is impressed by Brunson, admires Brunson, or has respect for Brunson.

Question	Answer	Common Core Reading Standard
1	B	Determine the meaning of words and phrases as they are used in a text, including figurative, connotative, and technical meanings.
2	C	Trace and evaluate the argument and specific claims in a text, assessing whether the reasoning is sound and the evidence is relevant and sufficient to support the claims.
3	A	Determine an author's point of view or purpose in a text and analyze how the author distinguishes his or her position from that of others.
4	B	Analyze the impact of a specific word choice on meaning and tone.

Food Poisoning

Core Skills Practice

Core skill: Trace and evaluate the argument and specific claims in a text, assessing whether the reasoning is sound and the evidence is relevant and sufficient to support the claims.

Answer: The student should give a reasonable example of specific information that could be added to better show how food poisoning can make people very ill. The answer may describe adding details about the symptoms of food poisoning, about the harm done by food poisoning, or about how people may need to be hospitalized or treated by a doctor.

Question	Answer	Common Core Reading Standard
1	B	Determine the meaning of words and phrases as they are used in a text, including figurative, connotative, and technical meanings.
2	C	Analyze the interactions between individuals, events, and ideas in a text.
3	B	Analyze the structure an author uses to organize a text, including how the major sections contribute to the whole and to the development of the ideas.
4	C	Cite several pieces of textual evidence to support analysis of what the text says explicitly as well as inferences drawn from the text.

Computer Health

Core Skills Practice

Core skill: Analyze the interactions between individuals, events, and ideas in a text.

Answer: The student should describe the purpose of comparing a booster shot with an antivirus program. Students may describe the similarities between the two, such as that they both prevent problems. Students may also generally describe how the comparison helps people relate to and understand the information.

Question	Answer	Common Core Reading Standard
1	C	Determine the meaning of words and phrases as they are used in a text, including figurative, connotative, and technical meanings.
2	B	Determine an author's point of view or purpose in a text and analyze how the author distinguishes his or her position from that of others.
3	B	Analyze the structure an author uses to organize a text, including how the major sections contribute to the whole and to the development of the ideas.
4	C	Analyze the interactions between individuals, events, and ideas in a text.
5	See Below	Cite several pieces of textual evidence to support analysis of what the text says explicitly as well as inferences drawn from the text.

Give a score of 0, 1, 2, 3, or 4 based on how well the answer meets the criteria listed.
- It should state an opinion of whether or not the student thinks it is important to have an up-to-date antivirus program on his or her computer.
- It should clearly explain why the student has that opinion.
- It should use relevant details from the passage to support the opinion.
- It should be well-organized, clear, and easy to understand.

Set 9: Literary and Informational Texts

First Day

Core Skills Practice

Core skill: Write narratives to develop real or imagined experiences or events using effective technique, relevant descriptive details, and well-structured event sequences.

Answer: The student should write a narrative that continues the story. The narrative should include details about what happens when Chris goes to attend to the event.

Question	Answer	Common Core Reading Standard
1	B	Determine the meaning of words and phrases as they are used in a text, including figurative and connotative meanings.
2	B	Analyze how particular elements of a story or drama interact.
3	A	Cite several pieces of textual evidence to support analysis of what the text says explicitly as well as inferences drawn from the text.
4	D	Determine the meaning of words and phrases as they are used in a text, including figurative and connotative meanings.

Amelia Earhart

Core Skills Practice

Core skill: Analyze the interactions between individuals, events, and ideas in a text.

Answer: The student should infer that the events would not be as significant today. Students may describe how flight has advanced, so flying across an ocean solo is no longer a remarkable achievement. Students may also describe how female pilots are not rare like they were at the time, so a woman flying a plane is not as significant or unusual.

Question	Answer	Common Core Reading Standard
1	B	Determine the meaning of words and phrases as they are used in a text, including figurative, connotative, and technical meanings.
2	D	Determine two or more central ideas in a text and analyze their development over the course of the text; provide an objective summary of the text.
3	A	Cite several pieces of textual evidence to support analysis of what the text says explicitly as well as inferences drawn from the text.
4	B	Trace and evaluate the argument and specific claims in a text, assessing whether the reasoning is sound and the evidence is relevant and sufficient to support the claims.

Poor King Henri

Core Skills Practice

Core skill: Cite several pieces of textual evidence to support analysis of what the text says explicitly as well as inferences drawn from the text.

Answer: The student should give an opinion on whether or not King Henri's friends would be understanding of his changes of mood. Either opinion is acceptable as long as it is supported. The student should support the opinion with relevant details from the passage, and may also include personal opinions.

Question	Answer	Common Core Reading Standard
1	D	Analyze how particular elements of a story or drama interact.
2	D	Compare and contrast a fictional portrayal of a time, place, or character and a historical account of the same period as a means of understanding how authors of fiction use or alter history.
3	D	Analyze the impact of rhymes and other repetitions of sounds (e.g., alliteration) on a specific verse or stanza of a poem or section of a story or drama.
4	B	Determine the meaning of words and phrases as they are used in a text, including figurative and connotative meanings.

A Helping Hand

Core Skills Practice

Core skill: Determine two or more central ideas in a text and analyze their development over the course of the text; provide an objective summary of the text.

Answer: The student should list three examples of Dr. Price helping people. Examples are given below.

      1. He helped doctors in Japan after an earthquake.

      2. He helped people in Africa living in poverty.

      3. He travels to schools to teach students about healthcare issues.

Question	Answer	Common Core Reading Standard
1	C	Determine an author's point of view or purpose in a text and analyze how the author distinguishes his or her position from that of others.
2	C	Analyze the interactions between individuals, events, and ideas in a text.
3	A	Determine two or more central ideas in a text and analyze their development over the course of the text; provide an objective summary of the text.
4	B	Analyze the structure an author uses to organize a text, including how the major sections contribute to the whole and to the development of the ideas.
5	See Below	Cite several pieces of textual evidence to support analysis of what the text says explicitly as well as inferences drawn from the text.

Give a score of 0, 1, 2, 3, or 4 based on how well the answer meets the criteria listed.

- It should state an opinion of whether or not the student thinks that Dr. Price is an inspirational person.
- It should clearly explain why the student has that opinion.
- It should use relevant details from the passage to support the opinion.
- It should be well-organized, clear, and easy to understand.

Set 10: Literary and Informational Texts

Tau Ceti

Core Skills Practice

Core skill: Use common, grade-appropriate Greek or Latin affixes and roots as clues to the meaning of a word.

Answer: The student should complete the table by writing a definition of each word. Examples are given below.

extracurricular	outside of normal studies
extraordinary	beyond ordinary
extrasensory	from outside the senses

Question	Answer	Common Core Reading Standard
1	C	Determine the meaning of words and phrases as they are used in a text, including figurative, connotative, and technical meanings.
2	D	Analyze the interactions between individuals, events, and ideas in a text.
3	A	Determine an author's point of view or purpose in a text and analyze how the author distinguishes his or her position from that of others.
4	A	Cite several pieces of textual evidence to support analysis of what the text says explicitly as well as inferences drawn from the text.

The Exam

Core Skills Practice

Core skill: Determine the meaning of words and phrases as they are used in a text, including figurative and connotative meanings.

Answer: The student should explain whether or not describing algebra as being "like a tapestry of symbols" is a good description. Students may have either opinion as long as it is supported with a reasonable explanation.

Question	Answer	Common Core Reading Standard
1	B	Determine the meaning of words and phrases as they are used in a text, including figurative and connotative meanings.
2	Asks Kevin for help Studies with his mother Gets tutored by Miss Bert	Determine a theme or central idea of a text and analyze its development over the course of the text; provide an objective summary of the text.
3	A	Cite several pieces of textual evidence to support analysis of what the text says explicitly as well as inferences drawn from the text.
4	A	Analyze how a drama's or poem's form or structure contributes to its meaning.

Constantinople

Core Skills Practice

Core skill: Conduct short research projects to answer a question, drawing on several sources and generating additional related, focused questions for further research and investigation.

Answer: The student should list questions that would be appropriate to answer in a report about what life was like in Constantinople.

Question	Answer	Common Core Reading Standard
1	D	Determine two or more central ideas in a text and analyze their development over the course of the text; provide an objective summary of the text.
2	B	Trace and evaluate the argument and specific claims in a text, assessing whether the reasoning is sound and the evidence is relevant and sufficient to support the claims.
3	B	Analyze how two or more authors writing about the same topic shape their presentations of key information by emphasizing different evidence or advancing different interpretations of facts.
4	C	Determine two or more central ideas in a text and analyze their development over the course of the text; provide an objective summary of the text.

Going to a Show

Core Skills Practice

Core skill: Analyze how particular elements of a story or drama interact.

Answer: The student should explain that Jacob felt good because he wanted to see his favorite band, but felt bad about having to choose which friends to take.

Question	Answer	Common Core Reading Standard
1	B	Determine the meaning of words and phrases as they are used in a text, including figurative and connotative meanings.
2	C	Analyze how a drama's or poem's form or structure contributes to its meaning.
3	D	Analyze how an author develops and contrasts the points of view of different characters or narrators in a text.
4	A	Determine a theme or central idea of a text and analyze its development over the course of the text; provide an objective summary of the text.
5	See Below	Cite several pieces of textual evidence to support analysis of what the text says explicitly as well as inferences drawn from the text.

Give a score of 0, 1, 2, 3, or 4 based on how well the answer meets the criteria listed.
- It should state an opinion on whether or not Jacob chose which friends to take fairly.
- It should clearly explain why the student has that opinion.
- It should use relevant details from the passage to support the opinion.
- It should be well-organized, clear, and easy to understand.

Set 11: Paired Literary Texts

The Old Hollow Bakery/The Highest Price

Core Skills Practice

Core skill: Cite several pieces of textual evidence to support analysis of what the text says explicitly as well as inferences drawn from the text.

Answer: The student should identify details that show that the bakery is popular. Students may describe how children rush in each morning or how the children like the treats. The student should identify details that show that Mrs. Dunn is a good baker. Students may describe how the food she bakes is described as fine, wonderful, and mouth-watering, or how people like the food she bakes a lot.

Core Skills Practice

Core skill: Compare and contrast a written story, drama, or poem to its audio, filmed, staged, or multimedia version, analyzing the effects of techniques unique to each medium.

Answer: The student should infer that Captain Ludikar would sound upset, stressed, or uncertain. Students should show an understanding of how Captain Ludikar feels.

Question	Answer	Common Core Reading Standard
1	D	Determine the meaning of words and phrases as they are used in a text, including figurative and connotative meanings.
2	A	Determine the meaning of words and phrases as they are used in a text, including figurative and connotative meanings.
3	C	Determine a theme or central idea of a text and analyze its development over the course of the text; provide an objective summary of the text.
4	B	Analyze how particular elements of a story or drama interact.
5	D	Analyze how an author develops and contrasts the points of view of different characters or narrators in a text.
6	A	Compare and contrast a fictional portrayal of a time, place, or character and a historical account of the same period as a means of understanding how authors of fiction use or alter history.
7	B	Analyze how a drama's or poem's form or structure contributes to its meaning.
8	C	Cite several pieces of textual evidence to support analysis of what the text says explicitly as well as inferences drawn from the text.
9	See Below	Analyze how an author develops and contrasts the points of view of different characters or narrators in a text.

Give a score of 0, 1, 2, 3, or 4 based on how well the answer meets the criteria listed.
- It should give a reasonable analysis of how Captain Ludikar and Mrs. Dunn have similar motivations.
- It should refer to how they both care about people, with Captain Ludikar caring that his colleagues are okay and Mrs. Dunn caring about making her customers happy.
- It should use relevant details from both passages.
- It should be well-organized, clear, and easy to understand.

Set 12: Paired Informational Texts

The Ambassadors/Michelangelo

Core Skills Practice

Core skill: Determine two or more central ideas in a text and analyze their development over the course of the text; provide an objective summary of the text.

Answer: The student should summarize how *The Ambassadors* is an example of anamorphic design. The answer should describe how anamorphic design means that images can only be seen from a certain angle and explain how the painting has a skull that only looks like a skull when viewed from the side.

Core Skills Practice

Core skill: Trace and evaluate the argument and specific claims in a text, assessing whether the reasoning is sound and the evidence is relevant and sufficient to support the claims.

Answer: The student should identify that there were no cranes or other machinery at the time to make lifting the statue onto the building easier.

Question	Answer	Common Core Reading Standard
1	D	Determine two or more central ideas in a text and analyze their development over the course of the text; provide an objective summary of the text.
2	B	Cite several pieces of textual evidence to support analysis of what the text says explicitly as well as inferences drawn from the text.
3	D	Determine an author's point of view or purpose in a text and analyze how the author distinguishes his or her position from that of others.
4	A	Determine the meaning of words and phrases as they are used in a text, including figurative, connotative, and technical meanings.
5	C	Compare and contrast a text to an audio, video, or multimedia version of the text, analyzing each medium's portrayal of the subject.
6	D	Analyze the impact of a specific word choice on meaning and tone.
7	B	Cite several pieces of textual evidence to support analysis of what the text says explicitly as well as inferences drawn from the text.
8	B	Analyze the structure an author uses to organize a text, including how the major sections contribute to the whole and to the development of the ideas.
9	See Below	Analyze how two or more authors writing about the same topic shape their presentations of key information by emphasizing different evidence or advancing different interpretations of facts.

Give a score of 0, 1, 2, 3, or 4 based on how well the answer meets the criteria listed.
- It should give a reasonable explanation of what makes *The Ambassadors* and the statue of *David* special.
- It should include that they are both special because of their details, with *The Ambassadors* special because it contains an object that can only be viewed from an angle and *David* special because it has been carved in such striking detail.
- It may also describe additional similarities or difference between the two artworks.
- It should use relevant details from both passages.
- It should be well-organized, clear, and easy to understand.

Made in the USA
Middletown, DE
21 September 2015